Paranormal Bedtime Stories

This is book one of a series

Todd Chapman

Paperback Print ISBN: 979-8-9874129-0-9

Kindle eBook ISBN: 979-8-9874129-1-6

Audiobook ISBN: 979-8-9874129-2-3

Contents

Testimonials

Who out there doesn't love spooky stories about mysterious beings and things that go bump in the night? Most of us have at one time or other had encounters with unexplained phenomena, whether or not we would admit it to others for fear they might perceive us to be nutcases.

In Paranormal Bedtime Stories #1, author, former UFO tour guide and lecturer Todd Chapman has assembled a collection of firsthand accounts from people unafraid to share their otherworldly experiences with his readers. This group of stories relates their personal experiences with Bigfoot, alien orbs and craft, invisible beings, ghostly manifestations and even a chupacabra.

If you're a fan of the supernatural, give it a read. There's something there for everyone. – Kerry S.

Paranormal Bedtime Stories is a fascinating compilation of eyewitness encounters with the paranormal, extraterrestrial, and other dimensional that have been shared with and/or experienced by the author. From Sasquatch sightings to visits from alien beings, these stories feature an array of paranormal activity and are thought provoking for the believer and skeptic alike. The author obviously possesses an energy that is open not only to having these experiences, but that makes people feel comfortable sharing stories of their personal experiences that could subject them to ridicule by some.

These stories really make you wonder how many people live among us who have had paranormal experiences and how many of them can not only detect when there is an other-worldly presence nearby, but also possess an ability to invite this presence to make further contact. I think the true number would shock us all. These stories inspire those of us with open minds to pursue more information, to keep searching for answers to the unknown, and to face our fears head on to possibly have an encounter of our own. A few of the experiences shared in this book made the hair on the *back of my neck stand up, but all left me eager to read more. I applaud the courage and insight of the author and those involved in sharing these stories so that we can try to understand the unknown aspects of our very existence. – Holly F.*

Acknowledgments

Not all of us have a paranormal story to tell, so I appreciate everyone who's shared their encounters in this book.

Likewise, I'm grateful for everyone who has, over the years, ventured into the unknown with me. Together, we experienced what many call the paranormal or supernatural, even impossible.

Last, I want to thank those unseen and seen that interacted with us.

Foreword

Telling a story is easy if the story you tell is something that happened to you. A first-person narrative of an event you saw and experienced comes naturally. You were there in that time and space and you will describe the episode with honest clarity. On the other hand, and for obvious reasons, relating something that happened to other people is more difficult. You try to repeat someone's words to replicate the emotion they went through, as well as the way the story made you feel. To deliver the details so that your audience is swept into the excitement or terror of that moment is not an easy task. I found this to be the case when I naively thought that starting a storytelling podcast would be easy. It's not.

My first podcasts were the retelling of stories I heard others tell through the years. While at lunch on a job site, for instance, someone would recount a crazy story about a ghost they saw. At a party there is always the person describing an experience with Bigfoot or a Demon or a weird UFO. For some reason, I remember these stories in great detail and can put them in writing to narrate on my podcast. Ask me to remember the birth dates of anyone in my family and I cannot, but tell me a story about an encounter you've had with other-worldly entities, I will never forget.

After uploading ten podcasts, I ran out of my own stories. I needed help, so in a plea of desperation, I asked my small audience to email their stories to me and that I would narrate them on my podcast. To my amazement, I received over ten emails that week. Only one of those emails was in literary condition to narrate. The others needed editing first, so I got to work. Over the years, stories sent by random people who regularly listen to my podcast are the meat and potatoes of my show.

In the winter of 2020, I interviewed a man from Colorado who claimed one or more Sasquatch harassed him and his family at home. The interview was popular and created a stir in the Bigfoot community. Namely, because the ordeal they endured was scary and traumatic.

To this day, I receive emails from people who want to hear more from him. I tried repeatedly to interview him again, but was unsuccessful.

On March 19, 2020, over two years after I started my podcast, and not long after the Colorado interview, I received an email from Todd, which caught my eye. The subject regarded that interview.

His email was fascinating, actually. It described an interview he did with some locals in the same part of Colorado. These people experienced similar events with a creature they believed was a Sasquatch. I included his story in my next podcast - *it was that good*.

It would be the beginning of a rich correspondence with a good writer who experienced some of the most fascinating things I've heard. Through his writing, I got the sense that Todd had a unique connection with the people he gathered stories from. I think he is also a good listener, and that makes for a great storyteller. I also believe he has the spirit of a child when he is a witness to the paranormal. I am sure he could be frightened, but like me, I believe he looks at these events in wonder, amazement, and curiosity.

Since that first email, I have included his stories in no less than ten podcasts. I admit, I am giddy when I see his name arrive in my inbox. I know that something intriguing awaits me. No matter how busy I am, I open Todd's emails to read the next in a series of stories that have heightened my imagination.

At some point, I remember telling Todd that he had a book on his hands. It did not surprise me when his response was that he had several books planned. With work and life, the process was slow. But the books were coming. And then the day came a few weeks ago when the manuscript for this book arrived. I read the fifty stories and was not disappointed with a single paragraph. It was like all of his emails, but on steroids.

Paranormal Bedtime Stories is a book title I would have never chosen. It crossed my mind to tell Todd he would have to change it if he wanted to sell books. However, after reading this book, I believe it is the perfect title, because this is exactly what this book is. These are short stories you will read in five to ten minutes at the breakfast table, on your lunch break, while sitting in traffic, or in bed before you fall asleep. The latter being the perfect time to read them. The stories will enhance your REM sleep and dreams, if not give you night terrors.

Paranormal Bedtime Stories is not a collection of fiction. These are true stories, which either he experienced or was told by others while in an environment and space, where they felt at ease. As you will see, he has a way of doing this out in the field in real-time, as it's going down.

You can read the Author's Bio at the end of the book to discover why Todd is uniquely qualified to relate these stories to us.

I enjoy novels and long form non-fiction, but since the start of my podcast I have fallen in love with reading stories in short format. When they are written as a story instead of something like a courtroom testimony, they will capture your imagination. You will enjoy this book for the sake of the story. In addition, the events in this book will leave you pondering the world around you. They are well written and will hold your attention. I suspect that when you finish one story, you will want to move to the next one, no matter if it will make you late for work or keep you up past your bedtime. That is the effect *Paranormal Bedtime Stories* has on me. As I write this, I am already looking forward to book two of this thrilling series.

In the first paragraph, I stated that telling a story is easy. However, *writing* a story is not. I don't know how difficult it was for the author to compile and write the events in this book, but he sure makes it look easy. Todd Chapman is a natural storyteller. You will agree as you turn the pages, so be prepared for something that could forever make you question if the world you live in is actually what you think it is.

Cameron Buckner
Host of the Dixie Cryptid YouTube Podcast

Introduction

Do you enjoy a good bedtime story? In this book, you will discover fascinating accounts involving aliens, bigfoot, ghosts, and more. This book is not meant to prove or disprove the existence of or the manner in which the supernatural or paranormal interacts with us. This is simply a collection of interesting stories. Like any good campfire or bedtime story, there will be plenty to debate with your friends and family.

Some stories in this book strangers shared with the author during his travels, while others came from people he knows, as well as from his experience as a paranormal tour guide. Over the course of his *Bedtime Story* series, Todd will include more and more of his own fascinating experiences.

It's the author's wish that you share these stories with friends while camping, during road trips, sleep-overs, and while on other adventures.

Also, if you enjoy falling asleep to good storytelling, you are in luck.

A few years ago, Todd found Cameron Buckner's Dixie Cryptid YouTube channel, and after listening to podcasts for a year, began submitting stories for the show. Many of the stories in this book are on the Dixie Cryptid channel. When this is the case, links to the podcasts have been added to a playlist on Todd's website. Simply go to the *Conclusion* page at the end of this book and scan the QR Code and enter the password when prompted. Alternatively, you can visit

www.ToddChapmanBooks.com

and click on *Podcast Playlist* from the menu. Enter the password on the *Conclusion* page.

To subscribe to the Dixie Cryptid channel for more viewer-submitted stories like those in this book, go to

www.youtube.com/c/DixieCryptid

or search YouTube.com for "*Dixie Cryptid.*"

If you have a story you'd like included on the Dixie Cryptid podcast, email it to **dixiecryptid@gmail.com**.

Now sit back and enjoy!

Chapter 1

His Name is Todd

Ghosts Show Themselves

F rom the first night they lived in the house, bumps or thuds, the sound of feet running in the attic, beings walking past windows, and the sounds of doors shutting, all began at 11:00 PM every night.

After a long tour, I'd often get back to their house well after midnight, even as late as 3:00 AM. I would drop off their truck and then drive my car home, which was a good 35 minute drive.

Already tired, it was common for me to spend the night on their couch rather than driving all the way home.

My boss's daughter always had friends staying over, even on weeknights. They were always up all night playing and talking in her bedroom.

One night while sleeping on the couch, I awoke to find three of them curled up together on the floor next to the couch. They hadn't slept yet, and the sun was on the rise.

I asked, *"What's going on? How come you're not in your room?"*

One of them said, *"We can't sleep in there."*

"What do you mean?"

"*We hear noises and see things outside the window,*" their daughter said.

"*What sort of noises?*"

"*Like people running on the roof,*" she replied. "*It always happens at 11 o'clock.*"

"*Okay,*" I said, as I rolled back over and went to sleep.

Over the next several weeks, this same thing played out again and again. Finally, her mother changed bedrooms with her. But that didn't help.

Then their daughter's birthday arrived, and they took her to Las Vegas. They asked me to house sit and keep an eye on the dog.

It was business as usual at the shop and I'd crash at their place afterwards. The dog and I got along great and when it was time for bed, she slept close by.

The first night, I heard THEM become active! The house was previously quiet and then sounded as if a family returned home from vacation or something. Doors were slamming, kids were running around, etc.

When I turned to see what time it was, the clock said 11:00 PM.

"*Just like clockwork,*" I thought to myself.

She was right. There was a lot of noise and it sounded like a bunch of people up on the roof or in the attic.

While I lay there awake, I listened to them and mentally followed their activities around the house and made notes of where I heard them.

The following night, I went to bed before 11 o'clock so I could send them a bit of an invitation.

As I lay under the blanket, I sent them a thought that if they were okay with it, I would like to see them.

"*My name is Todd and I'm watching the house and the dog,*" I said to them in my thoughts.

"*If you would rather not show yourselves to me now, maybe you could appear to me during my dreams,*" I added.

Sometime in the early hours, I heard someone near me whisper, "*His name is Todd.*"

With this, I awoke to see two women in period dresses, maybe from the 1800s, standing about four feet from me. One of them was facing me, while the other, who I believe was the one talking, was slightly turned to the side with her back to me as if looking at the other woman while she talked.

The more I tried to focus on them, the more I awoke and the less I saw them. Within about 5 seconds, I no longer saw them.

After this encounter, I never again heard them in the attic, and that was the only time I'd seen them.

Chapter 2

Stalked by Sasquatch

Boy Scout Survival Story

Have you ever shopped at REI, Sportsman's Warehouse, Bass Pro Shops, Cabela's, or a similar outdoor store? If so, take a moment and consider what it might be like to work at one of these stores and some of the strange stories you might hear from customers. In a way, it's actually a great place to engage people about their experiences and if they ever encountered something strange or unusual while biking, boating, camping, hiking, or hunting.

This story is about a 28-year-old man that walked into a Bass Pro Shops store in central Florida. He was looking for a new compound bow for the upcoming elk season. While chatting with the store's employee about prior hunting locations, big game and such, the customer opened up and shared a traumatic story that he'd never shared with anyone during the 12 years since it happened. He only did so after the employee admitted he believed in Bigfoot and actually saw one out west where he used to hunt. In fact, they'd both been to and hunted in similar areas.

The man's story took place twelve years earlier, when he was just 16-years-old and while hiking with a friend at the Philmont Boy Scout Ranch in New Mexico.

Philmont currently covers 140,000 acres of wilderness near the southern end of the Rocky Mountains.

He began, "*During our two weeks of hiking, we both put over 100-miles on our boots. We enjoyed the rugged terrain, lush meadows, thick forests, trout-filled streams, and hidden natural treasures. In fact, we were having a great time. Until we realized we were lost. Imagine being 16-years-old and lost within an area that large. It was crazy. The ranch land covers over 200 square miles and is full of all sorts of wild animals. Namely black bear.*"

To add perspective to their situation, in 1986, Philmont had five separate bear attacks on campers during a two-week period. In 2000, four more campers reported being attacked. And most recently, in 2010, a 14-year-old boy was sleeping inside his tent when a bear climbed onto the tent and bit the boy. There was even a version of this report that claimed the boy was drug out of the tent by the butt. He'd gone to sleep with a candy bar in his back pocket and that attracted the hungry bear.

This man continued his story, saying, "*During our second night of being lost, we had just finished making camp and had started a small fire. It was getting pretty cold at night, so we both wanted to warm up a bit at the fire before collecting more wood to get us through the night. That decision might have actually saved our lives.*"

"*While sitting next to the fire and contemplating our situation, we both realized we weren't alone. There, standing quietly next to a tree at the edge of our campsite, was a massive hairy creature. Where it came from and how long it had been watching us, we did not know. We didn't hear or see it walk up. As we both sat frozen in fear, I remember being unable to rationalize a way out of our situation, and even thought that we were going to die and nobody knew where we were. Besides, if we could somehow escape, we didn't know which way to run and for how long. We were lost. This thing was just massive, and we were sitting on the ground at a distance too close for comfort. In a manner of speaking, we were sitting ducks."*

The store employee jumped in with a question: *"What did you mean, that the decision to warm at the fire may have saved your lives?"*

"Can you imagine what might have happened if my friend and I left our camp in different directions and went into the darkness looking for firewood? What if the creature or creatures were out there waiting for us?"

"I see what you mean. Yeah, that could have been really bad."

He continued, *"I'm not sure how long we sat there looking at it without making a sound or making a move. Likewise, it remained there motionless, but we could hear it breathe. It must have huge lungs, with the sound it made breathing! I still can't get over how massive it was. I keep using the word 'massive', as that's all I can think of to describe it."*

The employee asked, *"So what happened? How did you get away from it?"*

"After a while, it simply turned around and walked deeper into the forest. Neither of us slept a wink."

"The whole experience from our trip and everything we thoroughly enjoyed up to that point has been, for the most part, forgotten. Or maybe 'replaced' is a better word. The confusion and fear, compounded with being lost so far from home, made us want to repress what happened. In fact, my friend and I never talked about what happened or told anyone. Until now, talking with you here."

"Man, that's a really crazy story! You obviously found your way back to civilization. How did you get back?"

"At first light, we broke camp and headed for the nearest high point and started climbing. We found some landmarks which were on our map, and that led us back to the main buildings and parking area. We were thrilled, but also mentally and emotionally exhausted. Neither of us has returned to Philmont or New Mexico."

"So, where are you headed with this new bow?" asked the store employee.

"I'm going on a solo hunt with a guide up in Idaho. I hear they have nice elk."

"Your friend isn't going with you, then?"

"No, he doesn't hunt. Actually, he doesn't get out that much anymore. He's got a family and a demanding job to keep him busy."

"Man, thanks for sharing your story and I'm glad you guys made it out safely. I don't know what I would have done in the same situation. Good luck with your hunt, too!"

This was an amazing story, but what you don't know is that the store employee has also been to the Philmont Boy Scout Ranch! What are the odds of that? Having a fellow hunter to confide in is great, but it's even easier when they've seen one of these creatures as well, and have even been to the area where you saw it.

Over the years, I've met Forest Service Rangers, rock climbers, and a handful of others who once worked at Philmont. I bet there are many more Philmont stories out there.

Chapter 3

The Boy Scientist

Human Looking Aliens

We were in the process of moving into the new store location and while taking down and dismantling the sign out front, a stranger approached me. He wanted to share a few stories with me, so I stopped what I was doing and listened.

This story begins when I was around 4 or 5-years-old.

I remember my parents taking me to a location with small hills surrounding the area. We went there often.

One day, while en route to the location, I could see up ahead a metallic disk-shaped craft sitting on the ground and people appeared to be working on it. I remember thinking that it was being built by these people.

Once we parked and got out, the workers asked me to come over and inspect the craft. I also recall walking around it and somehow knowing where to place my hand to open a door into the craft. When a door did open, I was just about to go inside when someone stopped me to ask my advice on some other matter.

That's really all I can remember. I don't even remember if I eventually got to go inside the craft.

Over the years as an adult, I've been plagued with those memories, and I even set out multiple times to find that place, but never succeeded.

I remember the tiny location with the hills well, but I cannot member anything beyond the surrounding hills or how we got there.

He told me he's also asked his parents repeatedly about it and where they lived when he was 4 or 5-years-old, but they've continued to withhold that information.

He concluded, "*Either they've been told to keep it a secret or they really don't know what I'm talking about. It's really rather strange.*"

His next story developed while he was on vacation.

He was out near two popular hiking canyons when he saw some strange lights in the sky.

From his experience, he told me he felt they were not conventional aircraft, so he wanted to start up a conversation with some people who were parked nearby.

"*Something was strange about them,*" he added, "*but I couldn't be sure what it was.*"

"*When I turned around to look at them again, they were gone and so was their vehicle.*"

He told me he recalled going home and later that evening, asking for a sign that those were, in fact, UFOs he'd seen over the canyons.

He clarified, "*My request was specific to the day, time, and location where I wanted to receive the confirmation.*"

"*When the time neared, I drove up to the lookout near the airport. There were other people up there, so I wasn't alone.*"

He added, "*Two of the people standing near me seemed a little odd too, so I turned to the man and asked what had drawn them to the lookout that day.*"

The stranger replied, "*We heard there was going to be a large sighting in the sky at sunset.*"

Because of the odd coincidence of what the stranger said and where he pointed, he turned and walked away.

"*He pointed to the same location I saw the lights,*" he added, "*and that freaked me out.*"

"*As I walked away, I thought to myself, that's enough of a sign for me.*"

"*Suddenly, I heard the woman who was with him say, well, I guess there won't be a sighting after all.*"

The following story was the final experience he shared with me.

After possibly feeling separation anxiety or to reassure himself that he wasn't crazy and that his memories of seeing craft and interacting with other beings were real, he again asked for contact and selected the time and location.

This time, I arrived at my preferred location a bit early and parked the car and waited. As the minutes passed, I grew restless.

Then, right at the prescribed time, an old, beat-up truck pulled up beside my car. It was driven by a woman.

I couldn't believe it.

There were so many other places to park. Why did she have to park right next to me?

Looking back at my watch, it was now past the requested meeting time and I became frustrated! I huffed as I reached for the keys and started up my car. As I backed up and shifted it into drive, I looked back at the mother and child one last time. It was at that moment the newborn sat up and waved goodbye to me.

It wasn't until miles down the road and about half-way home that I realized what just happened.

I replayed in my mind all the details from that brief period in the park, leaving me no choice but to conclude they were there to meet me, and I blew it!

They were setting up a sort of picnic, but it wasn't warm out and what mother would bring a newborn child out into the cold elements for a picnic? And the child was not dressed warmly either.

And what newborn baby can sit up on its own, lift its arm, and then wave goodbye while looking right at me?

He asked me this while shaking his head.

Chapter 4

Attacked by Unseen Creature

Researcher Clawed & Suffocated

"**B**e careful what you wish for, because you might just get it."

If the two men in this story didn't believe it before, they soon would!

One afternoon around 13-years ago, I was informed that a couple of guys were driving up to meet with me later that evening. They wanted me to take them out to a local hot-spot with the intent of video recording their experiences.

When they arrived, I was surprised at what I saw. Their camera was huge, like one of those TV News cameras. However, this one was equipped with night-vision and an infrared flashlight.

They told me they ran a popular paranormal investigation website and hoped to come home with some really great stories and video footage for their subscribers.

After showing me all of their equipment and explaining what it was used for, we climbed into my vehicle and began recording.

On the way to the highest elevation point of the evening, I learned the cameraman was terribly afraid of heights.

"*I can't even stand on a chair to change a light bulb without getting sick*," he said.

His friend laughed, "*Yeah, he has to ask his wife to do it for him.*"

After the laughter subsided, I asked, "*So, are you going to edit that part out?*"

They laughed.

"*All joking aside, it's getting dark fast, so let's pull over here and get the equipment ready*," I suggested.

Surprised at what I was hearing, I asked the camera guy what was wrong?

"*The infrared isn't working! I don't understand. The battery is brand new and worked just fine when I tested it before we left.*"

This meant they couldn't use the camera after dark. A bit of a misnomer, night-vision still requires light to work. Light, be it moonlight, a flashlight, car headlights, street lights, or in this case, their infrared flashlight, gets amplified over 30,000 times using a phosphorus tube. The phosphorus makes night-vision appear green.

"*Stranger things have happened*," I said.

"*I wouldn't worry about it. It will probably start working once you get back to your hotel.*"

While he was putting the camera away, I pulled out our night-vision goggles to see what was happening above us. This was just in time for them to witness three objects. Two of them appeared to be satellites, traveling north together with some distance between them. As they neared the point of being directly above us, a third object heading east raced by them at a very fast rate and intersected their path directly overhead.

"*That was pretty cool,*" they said.

"*It's a good sign. Okay, let's get going. We still have a long drive ahead of us.*"

We parked, and they checked the infrared again. "*Nope, it's still not working.*"

I took a minute to point things out and briefly explain what I had planned. As they had more of an agenda, I asked if there was anything in particular they were interested in doing.

The camera guy asked, "*Where are the buildings? Is there a way we can see them from here?*"

I pointed toward the east and said we can look around for a good viewing spot after I get the flashlights out.

While standing at the tailgate and pulling out the gear we'd need, I heard them commenting about something. They were no longer standing behind me. They'd found an opening in the fence leading out into a pasture.

I stopped what I was doing and went out to meet them.

"*What's wrong?*"

"*Do you feel that?*" asked the cameraman.

"*What do you mean?*"

"*It's weird. I feel like something's about to happen. Something is close to us, I can feel it.*"

All three of us looked around, but we couldn't see anything.

"*Oh my god,*" he said. "*My heart's racing and I can't breathe.*"

"*Let's get back to the truck,*" I said, while pulling his arm.

Once at the tailgate, he was struggling for air and said his chest hurt.

"*My skin is on fire,*" he exclaimed while fumbling to pull his shirt up.

I grabbed a flashlight and shined it on his stomach.

"*Oh, shit!*" his friend yelled out.

There were fresh claw marks going from his stomach to the right side of his body!

He was still having a difficult time breathing and couldn't see very well, so I grabbed my camera and took a photo to show him.

"*Look,*" I said while holding up the camera.

"*What the hell?*"

I gave him some water to pour on the wound. Shortly thereafter, he started breathing normally again.

"*Let me see your shirt,*" I said.

When he pulled it down, there were no cuts or tears in the fabric.

"*Did you guys see or hear anything out there?*"

"*No.*"

I said, "*Something or someone just attacked you good without lifting your shirt.*"

"*Do you want to call it a night and go back?*"

"*No,*" he said. "*I'm breathing better now, so let's stay a bit longer.*"

His friend asked, "*Are you sure? I'm okay with going home.*"

"*Let's stay a while longer.*"

"*I'm fine with that if you guys are sure,*" I said.

Taking a few minutes to regain his composure, I asked them if they were interested in a short hike up the hill so they could get a better look at the buildings. They wanted to do the hike, but the friend was wearing flip-flop sandals, so we had to go slow and easy. The cactus is everywhere out there and walking the desert hills at night is not easy.

No more than a minute into our hike, the cameraman, who was right behind me, said he couldn't go on. *"I'm going back to the vehicle."*

"What's wrong?" I asked, while still marching up the trail.

"I can't breathe!"

"What?" I thought to myself. This was odd, as I had literally just inhaled a deep breath of cool night air and thought to myself how wonderful it was.

When I turned around to talk to him, I saw that his friend had also turned back and was already at the bottom of the hill.

"What's wrong?" I shouted.

"I can't breathe either."

I followed them back to the truck.

"Man, what's going on?"

Both men said they felt a heavy pressure on their chest, which effectively created a feeling of being suffocated.

As it turns out, around ten years earlier, a few other people experienced this same feeling just a few miles away while hiking in a canyon. For them, it only happened in a small area of the canyon and could be repeated if they tried to continue up that trail.

In another instance, a couple of hikers were able to sense the presence of two large beings. These beings were invisible to the human eye, but somehow they could intuitively sense where they were and even their physical dimensions.

As they approached the invisible beings, the beings appeared to back up to keep a safe distance. They must have suspected the men could see them because they reportedly moved in a zigzag pattern while backing away. With each change of direction, the two men were able to follow them. Finally, once the perceived creatures were backed up against a cliff wall, the two men began to feel pressure on their chest and experienced the same feeling of suffocation. If they backed away from the beings, they said the pressure was released and they could breathe freely. They said they tested this by moving closer and closer, then backing away repeatedly.

The men later gave a friend of theirs a map and directions to the location of the cliff wall. When she arrived at the spot, she said she also felt the pressure on her chest, but she didn't sense a presence when entering the area like they did. She only felt the reaction to being too close to them.

One of these men was a friend of mine, so I asked him if, to his knowledge, this suffocating experience was ever reported outside that canyon. He said no, he wasn't aware of any other locations. I then told him it just happened to the two guys who were with me.

Getting back to my two guests, now they had enough and wanted to call it a night. I asked them to come by the shop the next morning and I'd have a copy of a video for them. Earlier that night, they asked for some footage they could use on their website. Unfortunately, the video I gave them was the only footage they took home with them.

The next morning, I saw them pull up and went outside to greet them.

"How do you guys feel?"

They said, laughing, *"We can breathe better down here."*

"How's that scratch?"

"You won't believe it," he said, while lifting up his shirt.

"It's completely healed!"

"Whoa! That was fast."

"Tell him what else happened," his friend said.

I interrupted, *"Let's first go inside and sit down, then you can tell me."*

The camera guy went on to say, "*After we got back to the hotel, I developed a sudden urge to climb up on the balcony railing and jump!*"

"*Well, obviously you didn't jump, because you're here now,*" I joked.

"*That urge was stronger than anything I've ever experienced, but I was able to resist it!*" he continued.

His friend added, "*I had a similar experience while we were out with you last night.*"

"*What do you mean?*"

"*It was a very compelling urge, like someone or something was calling to me from the house. It was in my head, asking me to come inside.*"

"*Dang, why didn't you say something last night?*" I asked.

"*We already had the wind knocked out of us and he got clawed, so we just wanted to go home.*"

"*Yah, I understand.*"

Then the camera guy got up and walked over to me.

"*Look at this,*" showing me his watch. "*I discovered around three hours of missing time this morning.*"

His friend chimed in, "*Yeah, it's weird because the watch is actually adjusted behind by three hours. It's like he went someplace that's three hours behind and maybe while there, reset the watch to the current time.*"

I thought about it for a moment. "*Right. People with missing time don't normally report the time being adjusted like that. They have the feeling or knowing that something happened. Like they went to the store around noon and got home when it's dark outside. The clock stays the same.*"

"*And that's not all,*" added the cameraman. "*You were right! As soon as we entered the hotel room and unpacked the camera gear, the battery for the infrared light worked just fine.*"

We all laughed and shook hands.

"Thanks for coming up guys, it was great meeting you and I hope you can salvage something to share with your subscribers!"

I learned later that when they got back home, they found their website offline. They told me it crashed the night they were out with me!

***

This is the end of their experience, but not the end of the story.

Allow me to ask a question: Do you believe these men were victims in any way? If you do, remember that they said they operated a "Paranormal Investigation" service and even said they hoped for some interesting stuff to happen to them so they could share it with their followers. And actually, that's the entire reason they took time away from their work and families to drive up and go out with me that night. They wanted my help in making that happen.

So, they were actually successful. They returned home with a lot to tell people about. Their camera stopped working for no reason. Their website crashed. One guy was clawed and suffocated by some unseen force, he was coaxed to jump from the balcony railing, and then he had missing time. Who knows what happened there? His friend also suffered from suffocation and was being spoken to in his mind to trespass and go inside a deserted building in the middle of the night.

Now allow me to ask another question: Could there have been another reason for being coaxed up onto the railing? Other than to jump, that is?

Remember, he was terribly afraid of heights and couldn't even get up on a chair without getting sick. What if it was really an effort to get him up on the railing, but NOT to jump? What if he had been healed of his fear and getting him up on the railing was actually so he could see that he was no longer afraid of heights? Could that be possible?

The reason I bring this up is that people have been healed while there. It's happened so often, I honestly keep the idea in the back of my mind when crazy things occur and for no apparent logical reason. What follows are examples.

1. I've seen implants, yes implants, ejected or removed from two different people. The first was a 20-something year-old father, and the other was a teenage boy, while sitting beside his parents.

2. A middle-aged man was in a great deal of pain following an injury to his right shoulder while lifting heavy furniture. The pain grew and grew for a couple weeks and finally reached the point where it was keeping him up at night and he could no longer lift his arm. We went inside and he pulled back the collar of his shirt, revealing a small puncture wound in his shoulder. He said that while preparing to take a shower that morning, something caught his attention out of the corner of his eye in the mirror. It was a line of dry blood which had run down to his waist from this hole. If he pressed his fingers against the hole, he said he could feel the "track" of the incision or probe upward into his shoulder. Swinging his arm in full clock-wise and counter-clock-wise movement while laughing, he was obviously no longer unable to lift his arm. He also said there was no pain. He had absolutely no memory of what happened or who may have helped him with his need for relief. The next day, the hole had completely healed. Incidentally, his girlfriend was sleeping beside him that night and she had no memory of what may have happened.

3. A college student had such a great experience on his first trip out, where a weather vane began to spin very fast while he stood

underneath it for a photo. It spun for 60 seconds. There hasn't been power to that water pump for years and there was absolutely no wind that night, so being a student of meteorology, that was quite special. So special, in fact, he returned with a good friend who was pregnant. She suffered from severe anxiety and was fearful for her child's safety. I shared the story of the resident female Sasquatch visiting a pregnant mare in the corral every night. The mare gave birth to a healthy colt, while other horse ranchers in the area were having complications with births. Then I told her that the Sasquatch left footprints in the corral one day and beside hers were smaller, tiny prints. She had a child too. It was right after I finished this story, this woman cried out to the Sasquatch to help protect her and her child. Immediately, we all heard a powerful vocalization from the corral area, followed by an intense wave of love. We all felt it wash over and through us. That night, this woman was healed of her fear and anxiety.

4. A young man told me he was having problems with his marriage, where his wife didn't understand his interest in such things. He told her he wanted to come visit this hot-spot and surprisingly she said okay. Nothing happened during his outing and that depressed him, but he emailed me after he got home and told me a UFO had visited their home and actually hovered low above the house. She was home and went outside to see it, and now she believes and they have a wonderful relationship.

5. One woman told me that prior to his death, she was not on speaking terms with her father, so the evening for her was about making contact with him and healing unresolved differences and guilt she had been carrying since childhood. His spirit visited her,

and she recognized his smell and presence when he was beside her. She felt his love and found forgiveness and healing that night.

6. My landlord even went with me one evening and had quite the experience. This is how she described it:

As I began to step from the edge of the forest, quite plainly, I heard a voice right alongside of me that told me I no longer had to see anything and to just believe THEY were there. I stopped dead in my tracks – I couldn't move.

In the blink of an eye, my vision completely left me and total darkness absorbed me and somehow I felt my feet leave the ground. What immediately followed was a floating sensation.

I screamed for Todd, who instantly grabbed my arm, which seemed to pull me back to Earth.

Todd, I can't see!

"What do you mean you can't see?" he asked.

My vision is gone. Hang on to me!

He did so.

We stood there for what seemed an eternity to me, waiting for my vision to return. It eventually did.

Todd suggested we head down to the corral.

No, I'm not supposed to go any further.

He didn't understand until I told him what I'd heard. That THEY were there, and that I didn't need to see them. That I was just supposed to believe. He understood perfectly.

We turned around and headed back up the hill, through the woods at the top, and back down the other side. As we reached the last descent, I heard footsteps snapping and sloshing behind me. I stopped and listened. The footsteps got closer and finally stopped next to me.

I told Todd that someone was following us.

"I know," he replied.

We headed for home. My dreams that night could not be explained. I didn't even try. I just went with the flow and accepted everything that happened.

During the course of the following morning, I grabbed my large outdoor watering can, filled it to the brim (at least 10 pounds of water in it) and began to water the multitude of plants throughout my home.

Something seemed different. I stopped and tried to figure out what it was, but kept watering the plants.

Lifting the heavy can up to water a waist-high plant, I suddenly realized that the watering can was in my right hand. There was no pain whatsoever as I carried and lifted it for the next half an hour. I couldn't believe it!

For some reason, my right forearm had bothered me for quite some time, to the point I could not pick up a glass of water without such pain and almost dropping it. Many people had worked on it, but it continued to be a mystery for almost ten or eleven months.

That was 12 years ago, and I still have no pain. Someone had fixed me, I felt strongly, as a gesture of simply believing. Whatever happened to me out there that night, I'm still in awe.

These are just a few of the healings which were made possible, being at the right place at the right time.

So could the camera guy have been healed? Possibly, but I lost touch with him over the years and never found out. I often wonder about his friend, and the reason for his being called to visit the house that night. What could have been in store for him?

In both instances, these men were able to resist that beckoning, as though they had been given a choice and they chose to say no out of fear. What would you have done?

Chapter 5

Motel Room 119

Chased Out by Coyotes

*I*t *was New Year's Eve, 2009.*

After reaching our destination, a group of us stood beside the fence talking. Before long, one couple broke off from the group and pulled me to the side with them. We walked down the fence line so they could talk with me in private.

They informed me of their plans to return later that evening after the tour was over, and that coming out with me was about showing them how to get there. I asked them that if anything was to happen, they contact me. I also wanted to see their photos in case anything was to appear in them.

Before we rejoined the group, the husband snapped a flash photo of a corner where two fences met and where we were talking. In that photo was a silhouette of a man invisible to the human eye. He was on the other side of the fence and appeared to have a cigarette or toothpick in his mouth.

This reminded me of a photograph taken in that same location back in the 1990s by the previous homeowner. In their flash photo, a humanoid figure was leaning against the fence. His face looked flat and he had large, yellow eyes.

Was this the same guy and was he listening in on the conversation about them sneaking back later that night? You know he was, and boy, did he have a surprise waiting for them!

We drove back to the shop and everyone said goodbye. A few days later, I received an email from them.

The husband wrote:

While standing close to where we took the photo of the invisible guy earlier that night, my wife felt her hair stand on end.

"Something or someone is right behind me," she told me, "and we need to leave IMMEDIATELY!"

As we began walking back to our vehicle, we felt someone following us. Fear sank in and we quickened our pace.

Then, out of nowhere, we estimate a dozen coyotes were only a few yards behind us, forcing us into a full-on sprint back to the vehicle!

Those coyotes were so close, we could hear them panting right behind us at our feet, but when we turned to look, we saw nothing. This freaked us out, so we started running as fast as we could!

We made it back to the truck in one piece and never saw those coyotes. We raced back to the motel. It was around 1:30 AM.

At 3:00 AM, the walls of our motel room began shaking violently, lasting over 10 minutes! At first, we suspected someone next door banging on the wall, but we heard no one talking. This was unusual because for the whole week we always heard conversions on both sides of our motel room. The walls seemed thin, so this made little sense.

The next strange thing happened the following day, this time around 5:00 AM. From the same motel room, we heard a loud humming sound throughout our room for almost 30-minutes. It was strange because when we walked outside, we didn't hear the sound. As soon as we walked back into the room, it was loud again. We suspected it was a washing machine or something. When we checked the laundry room, it was on the other side of the motel and the sound we were hearing was only in our room.

Before checking out, we asked about noise complaints from other guests, but nobody else heard noises either night.

When I visited their motel to see if room 119 had a history of poltergeist or other paranormal activity, they said that it used to. But because the attendant hadn't heard of any recent activity, she believed it must have been some time ago since the last haunting.

Honestly, I don't believe the motel was haunted. I wanted to check to see if there was a history in that unit.

I also think someone out at the ranch had a bit of fun with them and kept them from getting a good night's sleep. After all, they were the only people ever to admit being up to no good and wanting to go back and look around when nobody was looking!

"You keep us awake, we'll keep you awake..."

Chapter 6

Don't Touch the Roses

Pissed Off Ghost Gets Revenge

Our story begins with a couple, who upon moving into their new rental home, decided to do some landscaping out by the pool.

After discovering a rattlesnake out back and with their pool party coming up, they focused on other backyard hazards.

That's when they noticed the overgrown rose bush next to the fence. The thorny bushes extended dangerously close to the swimming pool.

The renters talked about cutting them back and even digging up some roses so the yard looked more presentable and spacious for parties and other pool-side fun.

With her snippers in hand and about to begin, the girlfriend felt the need to stop and go inside the house. After she put her tools down and went inside, she accepted the roses as they were and no longer wanted to kill them.

"*What's wrong?*" asked her boyfriend.

"*Nothing. I want to take a break for a minute,*" she replied.

That was a lie, and she knew it, but she was trying to understand what had happened.

Interestingly, he too thought to leave the roses alone, but continued chopping and cutting until he felt the job was done.

The following day, a series of strange things began happening inside the house. In particular, after sundown.

The strangeness included overhead room lights turning off and on all by themselves. Flipping the switch didn't turn them back on/off and neither did replacing the light bulb when it blew out. The temperature in the room would also drop or rise to where he was so uncomfortable he wanted to go to another room.

This continued for a time before they concluded he was being harassed. But why? Was the house haunted?

They had recently moved into town, and this was their first house. Before living there, they never had this sort of thing happen, so they weren't sure what to do.

Their experiences sounded like classic poltergeist material.

He heard things and felt someone hit him during his sleep. Lights either blew out or flipped on and off and temperature drops, and sometimes spikes, forced him to leave the room. Items such as his sunglasses and car keys always went missing, too.

Someone seemed to have a bone to pick with him, and only him.

They soon got the feeling someone didn't want him getting comfortable in their home. His girlfriend was fine and had nothing happen to her or in the room she was in.

Then the opportunity arose to discuss their situation with the landlord.

They learned that the landlord's wife died while living there and is why he moved out. He needed something smaller and different, not reminding him she was gone.

They detailed all the strange things happening, but he didn't know what to say. He had nothing happen to him before or after she died.

That's when it occurred to the girlfriend that it was because of the roses.

She interjected, "*Maybe that feeling I had to stop destroying the rose bushes came from her? Maybe she was trying to tell me to stop cutting.*"

The landlord replied, "*She loved those roses and spent many hours a day taking care of them. They were here babies!*"

"*What do you mean? You said you were just going to take a break,*" her boyfriend said.

"*I know,*" she replied. "*I didn't understand it.*"

"*I wish you would have told me,*" he said. "*I also thought about stopping, but continued pruning.*"

After returning home, the paranormal activity continued.

Because of his transgressions, they took the hint to get out. Apologizing didn't seem to matter at that point. The departed wanted nothing to do with him.

The couple found a nice place across town and moved out as soon as they could. How nice was the new place? As they discovered, not that nice… but we'll get to that in a minute.

Right now, I'd like to share another story about roses that a tour guest shared with me one evening.

She shared the following experience with me:

While living in Stanton Island, NY, my husband and I had just purchased a home. It was August, and working at an area school, I had the summer months off during summer break.

On a random day, I decided to tackle some yard work out back. The yard had apparently been neglected for some time and I got a little clipper happy, whacking away at anything that looked like a weed.

As I approached a tiny rose stem, I smelled a very strong perfume scent. It smelled like a perfume a woman over the age of 70 might wear. The weird part about it was that none of our neighbors were around, so the smell literally appeared from nowhere.

I took it as a sign from the woman who used to live in the house that we should leave the little rose stems alone. The rose stems were scattered all about the yard, too.

What made me think or feel that way? I didn't know, but the message was pretty strong within me, so I left them alone.

Flashing forward to mid-October, while raking leaves one Saturday afternoon, there I saw among the dead and decaying leaves the most perfect and beautiful rose I'd ever seen!

It was especially weird because, from what I knew, roses didn't bloom in the fall in New York City. My thought was that the woman who lived in the house prior to my husband and I thanked me for saving her roses.

Now, getting back to our couple and their next home, they experienced many paranormal things there, too. This time, though, his girlfriend was included and so was her daughter. In fact, everyone who spent the night in this house came away with their own stories and lots of them!

What follows are some of those experiences.

1. **Porcelain Dolls:** The daughter collected porcelain dolls and displayed them atop her dresser, which was located inside her closet.

You may already know, many people have reported these types of dolls to be haunted or possessed.

In this case, there was one particular doll in her collection that did strange things.

Once, the doll fell over all by itself and lay motionless for a while before it sat back up. The three girls who watched it do this ran out of the room screaming.

More than once, their daughter heard a thumping noise from inside the closet and when she opened the doors to see what moved or made the noise, she found all of her dolls on the floor below the dresser. Well, all but one. Looking back at her was that one doll. Did it push the others off the dresser?

2. **Soccer Ball:** Their daughter signed up for her school's soccer team and one night, ran down the long hallway dribbling the soccer ball between her feet. She kicked it at an angle and it bounced off the wall and into her mother's bedroom.

When she rounded the corner to enter the bedroom, the ball rested at the base of the sliding glass door on the far side of the room. She couldn't help but notice a reflection in the glass of a girl wearing a dress. She didn't know what to think. She looked down at herself to confirm what she was wearing - shorts and a t-shirt, not a dress.

She took a couple of steps backwards without taking her eyes off the girl. The girl in the dress then bent over, touched the soccer ball, and rolled it out to her.

A little while later, she found me and told me about it. For whatever reason, she didn't talk to her mother about this sort of stuff. Once she went back to her bedroom, I told her mother.

Her mom chuckled in disbelief. *"She's just pulling your leg."*

This was why she didn't tell her mom about things happening in the house.

The next morning, her mom pulled me aside and told me she was up all night and couldn't sleep.

When I asked what kept her awake, it wasn't because of the soccer ball story.

She told me that someone was in the corner of her bedroom by the sliding glass door and was flicking the vertical blinds all night, only a foot away from her head. She looked in the corner, but didn't see anyone.

She added that she first suspected wind coming through the window to be to cause, so she got up and made sure the windows were closed. Nothing was open, and she didn't feel a draft.

Then she got up and went through the house to check the sliding glass door in the living room and the one in the dining room. All of them were at the back of the home and all were locked. Also, none of the other blinds moved like the one in her bedroom.

It was like a child trying to aggravate her by flicking her finger against the vinyl blinds, and saying, "*You still don't believe I'm here?*"

3. **Disappearing Snake:** While cleaning out the garage one afternoon, the boyfriend discovered a bright yellow and red striped snake. It was alive in his hand. He called us out to look at it. While doing so, it vanished right before our eyes. Actually, we were all within 2-4 feet away when it disappeared. I was closest to it. There was no pop sound. It just vanished from his hand like it blinked out of this reality.

4. **All Girls Felt Sick:** Once more, the daughter came to talk to me.

Her friends and her were feeling sick that day and a few minutes before she came to talk with me, someone entered her bedroom through the closed door.

She said, "*This person actually came through the closed door and stood inside my room. All three of us saw him. He was tall and bald looking, but he didn't appear to look human exactly like us. After he turned around and left the room through the closed door, we all felt better and felt fine the rest of the night."*

5. **Laughing Woman:** A woman laughed in the hallway outside the bedrooms. More than one person heard her and it happened more than once late at night.

I asked if it was the girl seen in the reflection, but it sounded like an older woman, not a young girl.

6. **Wood Snapping:** One of the store employees was sleeping on the couch when she awoke at the sound of someone snapping pieces of firewood behind the house. The sounds then entered the dining room without someone first opening the sliding glass door and she swore someone walked right by her to enter the kitchen.

Terrified, and as bravely as she could, she called out the name of the homeowner, but there was no answer. She covered her head with the blanket and struggled to get back to sleep.

Might this have been the same older woman heard laughing down the hallway?

7. **Confused Girl:** Again, I was sitting in the backyard next to the fire pit with the dog when their daughter and a couple of her friends came out to join me. They wanted to talk.

They told me a girl was in her room and looked confused. It wasn't the first time she appeared.

The next time she saw her, their daughter asked her what was wrong and the ghost girl responded, "I'm waiting for my family to come home. I don't understand what is taking them so long."

The following evening, during the daughter's dream-time, she somehow ended up in a kind of waiting room where a family was sitting down on a bench along the wall.

"*It was like a hospital waiting room or something,*" she told me.

While there, she learned that the waiting family was her ghost girl's family, and that they were already dead.

A couple of nights later, the ghost girl reappeared in her bedroom. That's when she told her what she'd seen and that they were waiting for her.

Then, the unexpected happened. The family appeared in her bedroom right beside the ghost girl. They all smiled back at her and then faded away. That was the last time she saw any of them.

Note: This ghost girl was not the same girl she saw in the reflection with the soccer ball.

8. **Alien Crashes Backyard BBQ:** The events that follow took place three days into a five-day spree of paranormal activity.

That evening, we closed the store early for an old-fashioned back-yard barbecue. We invited other researchers, friends, and employees.

After dinner, we gathered inside to watch a slideshow of photographs by one of the researchers. It was like a mini presentation about UFOs and aliens with a question-and-answer session at the end.

Having given time for the sun to set and the night sky to darken, it was time to go back outside and sky-watch using our night-vision goggles.

Several satellites flew by overhead, but the spectacle was only beginning and it wasn't limited to the night sky.

We did a group photo with everyone gathered together in the backyard's darkness.

Placing a camera up to night-vision goggles allows us to take photographs in the near-Infrared light spectrum. This spectrum is invisible to humans. The first photograph contained a two-legged visitor we couldn't see.

We were not alone. In examining the photo, you can make out a figure behind the second person on the left.

The figure had what appeared to be a heart-shaped head. I knew the second person from the left to be in touch with a group of extraterrestrials, so this didn't surprise him. However, it stunned the rest of us.

As amazing as that was, it wasn't the only revealing photograph.

Several other photos show the being's left hand. Four fingers were visible over the shoulder of the man.

Using the flash on another camera revealed two large orbs. They were a bright, solid red color and appeared to be floating close to one another near the group.

9. **Hand Print on Body:** Their daughter awoke one morning with a strange hand print on her body. This hand looked familiar to everyone that saw the photos from the backyard BBQ. It also stayed on her body for a couple of days before disappearing.

Chapter 7

The Mormon Monster

Fishermen Encounter Beast

W ithin a few minutes after Bass Pro Shops opened, an off-duty police officer approached the counter in the hunting section. The store employee took one look at him and smiled, saying, *"I like your shirt."*

"Thanks," the man replied. He smiled back, admitting that he gets that a lot. He was wearing one of those *Bigfoot is Real* t-shirts.

"Have you ever seen one?" the employee asked.

"No, but I have friends who have. I trust their judgment, so their word is good enough for me. Do you believe?"

The employee looked over his shoulder before responding, *"Yes, I've seen one before and I have a friend out west who's had encounters."*

The officer nodded his head, then lowered his voice.

A friend and I were bass fishing from my boat in a small lake not far from here. We were the only ones out there and as we worked our bait along sunken trees in the deeper water, my buddy asked if I'd ever explored the Mormon land. I said no, but have thought about it. That's when we first heard it.

Behind us and to our left, we heard large branches snapping. My friend and I looked at each other and then back toward the noises. The sounds were coming from within a wooded area on private land owned by some Mormons. We don't know if it's owned by the church or someone within the church, but the area comprises thousands of acres, and we never see anyone on that side of the lake. We refer to it as the Mormon land.

Anyway, the noises didn't last long, maybe a couple minutes, then stopped. My friend and I discussed what could have made all the noise as nobody would likely be on that land. Well, at least not that close to the lake.

After about 10 or 15 minutes of working our way closer to the beach, we listened for the smallest of noises, but didn't hear or see anything. My friend looked at me and asked if we should go look.

That's when all hell broke loose!

Sudden and deafening crashing sounds, followed by ground rumbling thuds and audible grunts. Then the snapping of large branches resumed with what sounded more like trees crashing to the ground!

We both sat there frozen in shock and didn't notice that we were still moving closer and closer to shore. At that point, the boat was within 100 feet from the beach. Our minds tried to process what was happening, but neither of us saw anything moving until a huge tree stump came hurtling out from the woods towards us! It must have been 20-30 feet up in the air before crashing into the water a couple of boat lengths from us. Whatever or whomever was in there was strong enough to throw a stump that likely weighed several hundred pounds about 80 feet towards our boat!

Can you imagine the sound a huge root-ball would make crashing into the water like that? I can still hear it in my mind, as well as remember the sight of it flying.

He added, *"There's only one thing that can do that."*
The employee nodded and asked if they saw the Bigfoot.

"No, but we both wish we did. It would help to better frame the event, you know, by knowing what it was."

"We've gone back to fish several times since then, but haven't had anything more happen. Friends have asked if we've ever gone back and into the woods to check things out. We have not and to be honest, I'm not so sure we should."

"*What do you mean?*" asked the employee.

"*It wasn't until we discussed going ashore to look around that all hell broke loose. I don't believe in coincidences, so to me, it wasn't until we talked about doing so that we received the reaction we did. What would happen if we went exploring? I don't want to find out!*"

Chapter 8

The Implant

Aliens, Bigfoot, and Jesus

T he story I'm going to share with you was told to me by a good friend, one day back in 2008.

However, before I get to her experience, I need to just put this out there: You may be triggered by what you're about to hear! Just remember that she's sharing what happened to her as best as she could piece together and that with many aspects of her account, she was oblivious to what was happening until after the fact.

In UFO circles, a Close Encounter of the 7th Kind or CE-7, is commonly referred to as Human/Alien Hybridization. In other words, it's the creation of a Human/Alien hybrid being, using either sexual intercourse or via artificial methods. Typically, when you hear traumatizing accounts of Alien Abductions, it pertains to these "artificial" methods of extracting ova and sperm from those involved, to then be used to create a hybrid baby.

In Biblical circles, the idea of Aliens or Fallen Angels interbreeding with Human women is commonly discussed with references to the book of Genesis, Chapter 6, where Nephilim (Giants) and the "sons of God" (Angels) bore children with women.

"When man began to multiply on the face of the land and daughters were born to them, the sons of God saw that the daughters of man were attractive. And they took as their wives any they chose. Then the LORD said, "My Spirit shall not abide in man forever, for he is flesh: his days shall be 120 years." The Nephilim were on the earth in those days, and also afterward, when the sons of God came in to the daughters of man and they bore children to them. These were the mighty men who were of old, the men of renown."

"The LORD saw that the wickedness of man was great in the earth, and that every intention of the thoughts of his heart was only evil continually. And the LORD regretted that he had made man on the earth, and it grieved him to his heart. So the LORD said, "I will blot out man whom I have created

from the face of the land, man and
animals and creeping things and
birds of the heavens, for I am sorry
that I have made them." - Genesis
6:1-7 // The Holy Bible, English
Standard Version.

Now let's get to our story.

"*To the best of my memory*," she began, "*I don't remember asking for
this to happen.*"

After pausing to collect her thoughts, she continued, "*A short six
months after I moved into my new home, I awoke with strange cut marks
just below my bellybutton. They looked a lot like incision marks, but I
didn't understand where they came from or when I cut herself. The night
before, I slept undisturbed and if I had any dreams, I didn't remember
them. There was also no pain around the area of the cut.*"

The cut marks quickly disappeared by the following morning and
left no scar or sign that anything had happened.

"*If I hadn't noticed them the day before, I never would have known
something happened,*" she told me.

While visiting with a close friend a week or two afterwards, her
friend noticed something different about her and asked, "*Are you
pregnant?*" as she reached out to touch her on the stomach.

This friend was a well known local psychic and intuitive and
continued, "*Your aura is indicating that you're with child!*"

"*I didn't know how to respond,*" she told me. "*On the one hand, I knew
I couldn't be pregnant, as I hadn't been with anyone in quite some time.
And on the other hand, I respected her gift and didn't want to tell her she*

was nuts, but that's the only option that made sense, so that's what I went with."

"*You're crazy,*" I responded, while letting out a nervous laugh. "*I haven't been with anyone since I moved here.*"

And with that, they changed the subject and finally parted ways.

"*Over the days and weeks that followed,*" she said, "*I began feeling a very powerful connection to my son.*"

She told me that the feeling lead her to dig out an old photo of him, and then replace a flower photo she had framed on her desk with his photo. After not speaking to him for a lengthy period, she decided to reach out to him.

This was a difficult decision for her to make, as it was my understanding that after his birth, she chose to put him up for adoption to protect him from his abusive father, who didn't want him. She had since divorced his father, so that helped her feel a little more comfortable talking to her son after so many years. She had no idea what she'd say or if he'd even want to talk to her. All she knew, was that she was suddenly grappling with a very powerful urge to connect with him.

In the months ahead, she recalled seeing unusual weight gains as well. She ate healthy and told me, "*It just didn't make any sense. My lifestyle remained the same, but the weight just kept adding up. Nothing I did made a difference.*"

Then, one September morning while sitting at her desk at work, a man she didn't know entered her office while looking around for something or someone. When he noticed her, he said, "*You're the one…*"

Now that he had her undivided attention, he continued, "*Do you know you're implanted?*"

"*Where or in what area of my body?*" she asked out of curiosity.

He then made a circular motion in front of her stomach and said, "*In this general area.*"

He told her that he was in construction in Chicago and after receiving an important message for Hopi elders, he got in his truck and drove out to the Four Corners area of Arizona, New Mexico, Colorado, and Utah, to meet with them. On the way, he said he received another message and that he'd know who to give it to when he saw them. All he knew was that he couldn't meet with the Hopi until after passing on his second message.

He continued, "*I've been driving all over town and visiting shops looking for you!*"

"*I didn't know what to say,*" she confessed. "*I didn't know this man from Adam or understand why there was such a pressing need to tell me I was implanted.*"

From her understanding, implants were usually found behind someone's ear, in their sinus cavity, in a leg, the back of the arm, etc. Not in the general area of her stomach.

The strangeness of their meeting was added to her growing list of unexplained things, for which she had yet to make sense of.

She looked at me with a smirk, then continued, "*At this point, I still hadn't made the connection of implanted really meaning impregnated and all the hints I'd so far received.*"

"*Skipping ahead to September 2009, exactly one year after first meeting this construction worker, he returned with another message for me.*"

"*Did you know your implant was removed?*" he asked.

"*No, I didn't.*"

Unlike their decision to leave the cut marks behind when they implanted her, they left no sign of removing the fetus. The only hints would have come from her intuitive friend, her realizing those heavy maternal feelings were gone, or from someone like the man from Chicago.

Another struggle she had to deal with, was the biological loss after the fetus was taken. As a woman and as a mother, having previously navigated maternal and biological changes to support a new life, she later struggled mentally, emotionally, and physiologically with the sudden changes of that new life suddenly being taken from her. It was during this part of her ordeal, she began putting the pieces together.

Additionally, imagine how she may have felt knowing she didn't have a say in the matter. As with most if not all Abductees, there are still many questions to be answered. Such as, *"Why me?"*

Finally, no conversation about Alien Abduction or Hybridization would be complete without bringing up how Jesus was conceived. Even after generations of indoctrination, some people still refuse to accept that the Virgin Mary simply awoke one morning with child. Might there be another possible and even plausible explanation?

In the book of Matthew 1:18-25, it says:

> 18 Now the birth of Jesus Christ took place in this way. When his mother Mary had been betrothed to Joseph, before they came together she was found to be with child from the Holy Spirit.

19 And her husband Joseph, being a just man and unwilling to put her to shame, resolved to divorce her quietly.

20 But as he considered these things, behold, an angel of the Lord appeared to him in a dream, saying, "Joseph, son of David, do not fear to take Mary as your wife, for that which is conceived in her is from the Holy Spirit.

21 She will bear a son, and you shall call his name Jesus, for he will save his people from their sins."

22 All this took place to fulfill what the Lord had spoken by the prophet:

23 "Behold, the virgin shall conceive and bear a son, and they shall

call his name Immanuel" (which
means, God with us).

24 When Joseph woke from sleep,
he did as the angel of the Lord
commanded him: he took his wife,

25 but knew her not until she had
given birth to a son. And he called
his name Jesus.

The Talmud of Immanuel (The Teachings of Christ) is an ancient document discovered in Jerusalem in 1963. It was found in a cave encased in resin and had remained buried there for around 2,000 years. As this document in so many ways goes against long taught Biblical ideas and endless revisions, Church scholars and academia are largely opposed to its contents and claim it's a hoax.

One of their major sticking points, is that within the Talmud of Immanuel, Jesus Christ's biological father is identified as none other than Archangel Gabriel, returning us yet again to the debate of Angels being ETs, and the Fallen Angels being the negative ETs. [1] It also raises the question, again, of the validity of all those hybridization experiences reported by Abductees. For some, it's easy to deny their stories because of differing beliefs. For other people, though, it appears to explain in very simple terms how a woman

---

1. Talmud Jmmanuel - https://ca.figu.org/books2.html

such as Mary could awaken one morning impregnated with the Son of God.

If, over the years, you've heard accounts of Noah's Ark being located, chariots, spears, and bodies underneath the narrowest point of the Red Sea being found at the crossing point of the Exodus led by Moses, the site location of the burning bush, the cities of Sodom and Gomorrah, the tabernacle, golden calf worship, etc., those were by a man named Ron Wyatt and his sons in the 1980s. You can search on YouTube for all those incredible discoveries by Ron Wyatt and the full accounts.

Here, however, I'm going to touch on Christ's blood sample and how the test results relate to our story.

In early January, 1982, Ron discovered a dry blood sample in a cave beneath the site of Jesus' Crucifixion. The blood had apparently made its way through a crack in the rocks below the cross and dripped onto the Ark of the Covenant, which was hidden there in the cave and being protected by four men, who claimed to be Angels of God.

One of these angels instructed Ron to take a sample of the blood from the Mercy Seat and have it tested.

He did as instructed and took the sample to a trusted laboratory in Israel to be tested. The technicians knew nothing of the sample's backstory or who Ron was, just that they needed to test it to see if it was human. And it was. Per his request, they further tested it in a growth medium at body temperature for 48-hours, knowing full well that it was dead blood.

As Ron Wyatt says,

"Dry blood is dead blood. Everyone knows that. They can test the blood of the Pharaohs, the Mummies. There are certain things they can do.

They cannot get a chromosome count. There's no way I know of to get a chromosome count out of dry, dead blood. You can get DNA and some other things, but not a chromosome count."

"When the tests were complete, they said to him, Mr. Wyatt, this blood only has 24 chromosomes in it. Everybody else has 46. You see, 23 from your mother and 23 from your father. 22 autosomes from your mother and 22 autosomes from your father. You get an X from your mother and you may get an X or Y from your father. This blood had 23 chromosomes from the mother side and one Y chromosome only."

They continued, *"The child could not have developed if it didn't have the autosomes from the mother, so all of his physical characteristics were determined by his mother's side of the family. His maleness was determined by this one Y chromosome that came from a source NOT a human male."*

Then they continued, *"This blood is ALIVE,"* and asked him whose blood it was?

Ron answered, *"That's the blood of your Messiah!"* [2]

So, here we have test results showing a human mother with an unknown father counterpart.

In 2005, I met a woman who told me that many of her past lives had been revealed to her. Or maybe a better way of saying this, is that all of a sudden she had access to memories of different lives she's lived throughout time. Of interest here, is what she told me about her relationship to the Sasquatch species.

Like so many Abductees, she recalls vividly, laying on a table in a craft with beings standing over her. What is unique to her experience, however, is that she had been carrying the very first

---

2. Ron Wyatt Blood of Jesus - https://youtu.be/X67oUGc3qec

Sasquatch creation. After they removed the fetus from her, her only question was if she was good enough. In her case, she evidently knew she was playing a role in whatever was taking place.

Could this really be possible, though? Could this human woman be the original mother to the Sasquatch species?

Around 10 years ago, I heard a Blog Talk Radio interview with a man named Richard Stubstad. The show discussed DNA testing of a toenail and two other samples they believed to be from Bigfoot. All three samples were from various locations here in the United States.

The mitochondrial DNA or mtDNA results from our ancestral Grandmother (passed down from mother, to mother, to mother… over tens-of-thousands of years), revealed that samples #1 and #2 are similar to sub-glacial Europe or 15,000 years-old DNA data on record. Sample #3 is different, he said. Its mtDNA is believed to be upwards of 40,000 to 60,000 years-old and out of southern Africa. The male counterpart's Nuclear DNA or nDNA for all 3 samples revealed an unknown source. In other words, DNA analysis revealed the DNA from these random samples all had a Human mother component, while the father was unrecognized within all known genomes!

Richard Stubstad also stated that over the last 10 years, all evidence believed to be of Bigfoot DNA is 100% human in terms of female mtDNA. The male's nDNA in each instance is always unrecognized or unknown. [3]

As part of the ongoing Alien Abduction saga and contact scenarios, many female abductees report later being introduced to extraterrestrial children who they strongly believe to be their own

3. Richard Stubstad Bigfoot DNA - bit.ly/3Bupb6y

offspring. They even feel a very deep love for them, such as a mother would experience.

As of the time of this story, my friend has yet to meet her implant.

Chapter 9

A Hunter's Nightmare

Tracking a Lone Sasquatch

The following accounts come from the husband of a coworker. She knows about people sharing their strange stories with me, so asked if I'd like to meet her husband. What follows is an example of his strange and unexpected encounters while hunting.

During the second week of October, my brother-in-law and I arrived at our hunting location just after 5am. It was still a little dark out and I like to get out and just settle in to allow my eyes to adjust to the darkness before I head out. As I slowly made my way past empty homemade horse corrals, I was looking for an opening or clearing to just stop to look and listen. That's when I first smelled it. The odor reeked so bad, it was worse than any bear or mountain lion I've smelled.

That's when I felt like I was being watched. I slowly turned around and suddenly all the hair on my body stood up.

That caused me to chamber a round in my rifle and I also unsnapped my holster so I could pull out my pistol in case I needed to use it.

Suddenly, maybe 10-15 yards ahead of me, I heard a tremendous roar that was so loud it shook my entire body. The timber was dark, and it was still dark out, so all I saw appeared to be a large dark shadow. I could see it standing upright and moving just near the tree line. As I turned to look at it, it was looking at me. By this point, it was less than 25 feet from me!

As I knelt down to take aim at it, I couldn't find it in the scope. It was just too dark. While on my knees, I popped one of my Winchester 300 Magnum shells out of the magazine and onto the ground so I could retrace my tracks when it was light out. That's when the creature started moving down through the brush and trees toward the creek. When it took its first step, it was a long and deliberate step in the direction away from me. I could feel the ground shake when it took that step!

I quickly retreated the 300-400 yards back to my truck, where I found my brother-in-law still inside. He was hold-

ing his pistol up and close to his chest. I tried to open the door, but it was locked.

Open the door, I told him, but he shook his head and said no way! He'd heard it too and grabbed his gun. He said it made the hair on his body stand up straight as well.

We remained in the truck talking until after the sun started to come up and we could see better. It took some doing, but I convinced him to come with me to where I saw the creature. After we reached the spot, I located that Win 300 round and showed it to him. This is where it happened, and I pointed to a tree where it was. Now that it was light out, I could also gauge how tall it was standing beside a tree. Probably 9 feet tall, I told my trembling brother-in-law.

We could also see and follow its tracks in the grass, as it was so heavy it packed the grass down pretty good. So, we followed the tracks along the road for a while before I noticed that it curiously never stepped onto the road. It always walked along the side and in the grass all the way down to the creek, where the ground turned to really hard clay-like black dirt. You could tell it was really heavy when we could see its prints on that hard soil. That was an awful feeling!

The creature's tracks continued across the creek and up into the dark timber on the other side of the meadow. That's as far as we dared go!

As strange as it sounds, we continued hunting for the rest of the day, but didn't get anything. The next day, however, I had to remind my brother that we love hunting for bull elk and we could even see the elk about 400 yards to their east. He agreed with me, so we spent the day tracking elk, only saw cow elk.

While we were stalking the herd of elk, I told my brother that on the way back we could keep looking for sign from that creature, but he really didn't want to. He was still scared by its roar.

He continued that the following weekend, another hunter he knows well went hunting in the same area. In fact, the man's father-in-law owns the ranch they've all been hunting on and where these stories took place.

"*I didn't tell him anything about what happened the week before. This guy came back after the first day all scared, saying something was out there roaring and yelling at him. It evidently scared him so bad, he said he's never hunting again!*"

At this point, I interjected with the story of the team of men who were cutting fuel wood and left everything behind as they fled back down the mountain. He said that the location where it happened and where he's been hunting are only three miles apart, as the crow flies.

He proceeded to tell me about another incident, where he was scouting in an area not far from where the Sasquatch scared him and his brother-in-law.

"While hiking in an area where there are remnants of old gold mines from the mid-late 1800s, I noticed a deer stuck up in a tree. Its head was stuck in a wedge and its hindquarters were shredded apart. I looked for any sign of a mountain lion, but couldn't see any tracks, drag marks, or even claw marks the cat would leave struggling to get the deer up the tree. Nothing. So how did the deer get up nearly 15 feet into the tree and what animal shredded it up? Not picked at, but shredded."

"On another trip, a friend and I stumbled upon a large tee-pee structure made out of large trees. The two of us tried moving the smallest of the trees, but couldn't budge it. Then, in a more heavily wooded area, we found one twice its size. It would take a helicopter or heavy equipment to build such a thing. The trees were so huge."

He added that he has several friends who are veterinarians and taxidermists, and they want to go out with him to see what they can find, as he finds some really strange stuff.

"For example, during one trip, one of my friends discovered some strange hair. We had it tested, but the results came back unknown."

I told him about Josiah's hike, where he had the stones thrown at him while he sat inside a tee-pee. He knew that area well and continued with a couple more experiences from the same area Josiah hiked.

"While turkey hunting with my cousin, I told him that something down below was making a lot of noise, but I couldn't see what it was. Together, we decided to pack it up and venture down the mountain to where the loud thudding and grunting noises came from."

After adjusting in his chair, he continued, *"Near the creek, where the water had previously been high enough from the spring runoff to flood out a bit, and then recede, I found a large log that had recently been stepped on. When I saw it, I knew one noise I heard from up the hill was from something very large and heavy stepping on it. I heard it snap. Not crack like a smaller branch would make, but a loud dull popping or crushing sound. I could tell it came from a thick log that was snapped, and here it was. Part of it was stuck really deep into the ground. Something very heavy must have stepped on it and it had to be heavier than a bear, that's all I can say!"*

Again I interjected. Going back to the man who, after being yelled at by one of these creatures, said he was quitting hunting, I asked how many people he knows who have gone hunting in that area and had something frightening happen to them?

His answer was, *"I know about 5-6 men who were scared so bad, they quit deer and elk hunting altogether."*

Chapter 10

Little Yeti

Hairy Man Saves Baby Elk

I magine dining in a restaurant and overhearing someone's waitress say to another table, "*My nickname since I was a little girl has been Little Yeti!*" They'd apparently been talking Bigfoot when she walked by.

"*Wait, what?*" one of her customers asked as she was headed toward the drink station.

Their waitress turned back at them and smiled. "*I'll be right back.*"

After a few minutes, of which probably seemed like an eternity to those people, Little Yeti returned to their table.

"*What did you mean?*" asked one of the men at the table. "*Have you ever seen a Bigfoot around here?*"

"*Sure have. Many times. In part, that's how I got my nickname. I've sort of grown up with them.*"

The three people at the table just looked at each other with puzzled looks on their faces.

She continued, "*One morning when I was younger, I looked out the window of our family cabin as my uncle was outside playing with his two dogs. It was about then that he noticed they were nowhere in sight.*

After repeatedly calling their names, and also looking behind the cabin, he spotted them cowering under his pickup truck in the driveway."

"He called to them again, but they wouldn't even look at him."

"What's going on?" he wondered out loud. *"Then he noticed the direction they were looking was to the trees less than a 50 yards directly behind him."*

Everyone at my table continued to eavesdrop on the conversation, as their waitress paused for a moment and just looked at each of her customers.

The man in the green hat asked, *"Then what?"*

"Well, before my uncle even turned around, the hair on his neck stood straight up. He was almost too afraid to turn around."

"As he slowly gazed down at the dogs again to see if they were still looking behind him, he slowly reached inside the truck and grabbed his 30-06 hunting rifle. Once more, he checked with the dogs before he finally began to turn around."

Little Yeti stopped her story to add that the woods around their cabin have a long history of visitations by coyotes, black bear, elk, mule deer, bobcat, mountain lion, and if you believe some people, wolves and grizzly bear! Whatever was behind her uncle was scary enough to spook the dogs.

"My uncle cautiously swiveled his upper body towards the woods, holding the gun close to his chest. Then he saw it. Just our side of the trees stood a 7-8 foot hairy man, watching him and the dogs. He was covered in brown hair and stood motionless."

"I watched as my uncle slowly lifted the rifle to his shoulder so he could look at this man through his scope. Just as he put his eye to the scope, the creature turned and ran into the woods."

"Wow." said one of the men at the table.

"*Yeah, it took a couple minutes before his dogs felt safe enough to come back into the cabin.*"

"*Okay, can I get you all anything else?*"

Each of the three men at the table looked at each other, then one asked, "*So, why is your nickname, Little Yeti?*"

"*Oh, that's another story!*"

They all laughed and chimed in, "*We're not going anywhere…*"

"*Okay, but let me check on my other tables first. You sure you don't need anything else while I'm here?*"

"*Sure. How about another round of that delicious root beer?*"

"*Coming right up.*"

While she was away, the three of them just sort of looked off out the windows. Probably imagining what it would have been like to experience a Sasquatch up in the mountains. Especially when your two dogs are apparently unable to confront it. Seriously, many people go hiking with their dog, hoping it will help protect them. Maybe they would, but against a close encounter with a Sasquatch?

My friends and I looked at each other and smiled. "*Yeah, we're not going anywhere either. This is too good!*"

It wasn't long before their waitress returned with three large root beers.

"*So, where were we?*"

"*We're wondering where you got your nickname?*" said one of the men.

Laughing, "*Oh yeah.*"

"*The encounter I just told you about wasn't my first time seeing one of these creatures while growing up at my parent's cabin. In fact, I'd seen that particular Sasquatch many times before, so I'm not afraid of him.*"

"*My uncle, though, that was his first time. He'd heard some of my stories over the years, but never had a personal experience before. He didn't want to shoot it, just get a closer look.*"

She continued,

> *This will probably sound a bit unusual and maybe even unbelievable, but when I was 7 years-old, my parents and I were sitting in the living room of the cabin with the windows and front door open. It was about the same time of year as now, so having the windows and door open allowed cool air to circulate through the house.*

> *Suddenly, my mother said, "Listen, do you hear that?" We all stopped moving and tuned our ears towards the outdoors. "There! That, did you guys hear it?"*

> *We all jumped up and ran outside to get a better listen.*

> *My dad said, "That sounds like an elk calf calling out to its mother!"*

> *We all looked at each other and began moving towards the sound. It didn't seem that far away, possibly just inside the trees where my uncle saw the hairy man.*

When we arrived to where we thought the sound was coming from, my mother said, "It now sounds like it's over there, pointing to our left another 30-40 yards."

Once more, we stopped where we thought the sound was coming from, but we didn't see anything.

"There it is again," my mother said as she pointed back in the direction we were just at.

"What's going on?" my father said. "It's like it's moving around us, but we can't see it."

This continued for quite a while and before we knew it, we were quite a distance from the cabin. Then we heard the crying sound coming from the edge of a cliff. That cliff was nearly a mile from the cabin.

My mother said, "I don't get it. Where is the baby elk?"

My father walked to the ledge and looked down. "What the… ?" he blurted out.

"Come look at this!"

My mother and I ran over to the edge of the cliff and looked down to see what he found. There, on a small ledge, was a baby elk. Somehow, it became trapped about 25 feet down on a really small outcropping.

"Okay, so how would this elk get all the way down there without going over the edge?" asked my dad.

He didn't wait for an answer. "I'll be right back. I'm going for a rope. You two stay here and keep an eye on it."

My father disappeared back into the woods. Our cabin was now a mile away, so it would take a while before he returned.

My mother and I sat down on a fallen tree and just looked down at the baby.

Mom, how did it get down there and how could we hear it all the way through the woods to our house?

"I don't know, honey."

It didn't take my father as long to return as I thought. He appeared on the Ranger with ropes in the back.

"You'll never guess what I found on the way to the cabin," he blurted out. "The baby's mother is dead and her carcass has already been chewed on by coyotes. She's not far from here, over that way."

Dad tied up a rope to his harness and to a nearby tree, then lowered himself down to the baby elk. My mom and I stood above him and asked, "Can we do anything to help?"

I'm going to lift the elk above my shoulders and try to climb back up. I need you guys to keep the rope to the side of that tree root, so it doesn't get hung up. Okay?

"Yes honey," my mother replied.

It took my dad about 5 minutes to get the baby up to safety. He was exhausted and sat down to catch his breath. The three of us just sat there looking at the baby elk. It was probably relieved too, but didn't run off. It just lay down in the shade of my father.

The waitress stopped there, looked at her watch, and said she'd be back for the rest of the story. One of her orders appeared to be up, so she needed to take someone's food to their table.

"Poor baby," one of the guys said.

"Yeah. I wonder how this story ends," said another.

It was about 15 minutes before she returned to finish the story.

Okay, we have to hurry with the rest of the story. I have more tables coming in.

We all piled into our UTV and took the baby elk back to our cabin. I was the lucky one who got to hold it during the ride.

My dad slowed at one point and pointed up ahead. "That's the mother's carcass there."

My mother then suggested that maybe the baby ran for safety, but ended up over the edge.

"Maybe," said my dad, "but there's no way it should have landed on that small outcropping and not fallen into the ravine below."

Dad, do you know how we could hear it crying from way out here? I asked.

"No, I don't. A lot of this doesn't make any sense."

He continued, "For now, we need to figure out what to do with the elk."

We remained silent the rest of the way to the cabin.

"Bring the elk inside with you," my dad said, "as he took the machine out back and parked it."

Okay guys, to make a longer story shorter, the elk stayed with us until it was older. Much older! In fact, it was too large to stay indoors.

One thing became clear over time. The more and more we talked about the details of what happened, the more the only thing that really made sense didn't make any sense!

The cow elk was killed, and the baby needed shelter. There's absolutely no way we would have heard its cries for help at that distance. We even tested it by yelling and playing loud music from the Ranger. We couldn't hear anything that far out, even at night.

"So what are you saying?" asked one guy at the table.

"I'm suggesting that the brown-haired Sasquatch helped us find the baby. We also found large footprints near the ledge when we went back to test sound traveling to our cabin. That one Bigfoot came around a few times following our return with the elk. It was as if checking to make sure we had it home safely."

"Additionally, there's no realistic way the baby would have survived the fall 25 feet down to the tiny landing we found it on. We think that Sasquatch was mimicking the baby's cries to get our attention, and from a place we could hear it. Then it moved us closer and closer to the ledge where we believe it placed the baby. You know, so no predators could get at it."

The server stopped for a breather and let it sink in with her customers, who just looked at her.

"*Wow! That's an amazing story. But how did you get your nickname?*" one of them asked.

The server just smiled at him. "*As the baby elk needed to be taken care of and watched after, my parents started calling me Little Yeti, as I took care of the baby like the hairy man looked after it. Over the years, the name's just stuck.*"

Her customers just laughed. "*Yeah, that makes sense. Thanks for sharing your story with us!*"

"*No problem. There's more to the story and I have other experiences up at our family cabin, but have to get back to work. Have a great night and thanks for coming in for lunch!*"

My two friends and I just sunk deeper into our booth as we looked at each other and smiled. "*What a story, huh?*"

Yeah, I replied. Do you think it's true? I mean, do you think the Sasquatch really led them to the baby elk?

"*Why not? She even said there's more to the story. I can't even imagine what else happened!*"

Chapter 11

Werewolf Sighting in Texas

Drug Induced Hallucination?

While on vacation, a middle-aged couple decided to rent a 4x4 Jeep for a day-trip up the mountain. They rented Jeeps from my friend in the past, so they decided to stop by to say hello and see if anything was available. As luck would have it, he had a Jeep for them.

While filling out the rental agreement, they asked about one of their favorite restaurants a couple of blocks down the road.

He told them, *"It closed because the managers were way behind on rent and got in some trouble with the IRS. The owner returned and closed its doors. It's been for sale since."*

As it turns out, this couple knew the owner and, in fact, were his neighbors back in Texas.

My friend replied, *"My family purchased the lodge next to the restaurant from the same guy many years back."*

A life-in-the-past conversation ensued, and then they told him this unbelievable story.

"*Almost home one hot Texas afternoon, up ahead, we saw several official looking vehicles parked on the side of the road. We then saw a small group of men walking around in the field off in the distance. They were on our property and appeared to be looking for something.*"

They continued, "*Coming up to the stop sign, we recognized our neighbor among the men. We continued home and dropped the kids off before returning to see what was going on.*"

My friend asked, "*What was going on?*"

"*Evidently, our neighbor reported a werewolf walking upright through the field. The authorities came out to look for tracks or other evidence. Nothing was ever found.*"

In light of the strangeness of the whole thing, and this man's history of run-ins with the law, they suspect the incident was likely written off as substance induced hallucination.

My friend, like this couple, got a good laugh out of it.

When my friend told me the story, I did not laugh.

"*It could have been a dogman,*" I suggested.

"*What do you mean?*" he replied.

Up to that point, he'd never heard of Dogmen or their multitude of stories and sightings from Oklahoma and Texas over the years.

The area where this incident took place is in north Texas and not far from the Oklahoma border.

Even so, nobody will believe the man due to his criminal background and known drug use.

Chapter 12

A Texas Time Slip
Family Enters Alternate Reality

I t was 2009, when our family drove from our home in Houston, Texas up to a football training camp for our 9-year-old son. The camp was located in Austin, normally a 2-3 hour drive to our west. The drive had been fairly comfortable in our Mercedes SUV and we were making good time, with very light traffic on Interstate 10.

As we were therefore ahead of schedule, we decided to exit the highway for a small town to look for a place for lunch. That's when my son spotted a Whataburger restaurant. Pulling into the parking lot, we couldn't help but notice all the old 40s and 50s vintage cars and trucks. My husband commented that there must be a car show nearby or a weekend cruise going on.

When we walked inside and up to the counter, I noticed that the gal taking our order had hair and makeup that also looked right out of a 1940s or 50s movie. She was also very polite. Maybe even a little too polite. Her manners and vocabulary seemed strange. After we placed our order, we found a booth and sat down.

My husband commented on how all the employees seemed odd or that something wasn't right. He couldn't put his finger on it. We all turned our attention to the counter and kitchen area to study them more closely.

The men were not wearing polo-style shirts like we're used to. Their shirts were more of the polyester type and the colors were old-school, you might say. Of the two women, they were both wearing dresses, definitely not the usual top and pants uniform they wear in the big city.

As we discussed their attire, my son interrupted us, adding that we were the only ones in the dining room. That was odd, considering the 2 dozen or more vehicles in the parking lot and that they were the only business on that block.

Our name was called over the speakers, so my husband walked up to the counter to get our food. He asked the woman behind the counter where everyone was at, pointing to all the cars and trucks out front. She looked at him and then out the window, then just sort of looked back at him as if she didn't understand what he meant. Nothing more was said. My husband returned to the table and we blessed our meal.

I looked at my watch and decided we best be on our way. We thanked them for lunch and proceeded to our car. My husband commented that all the vehicles were empty and nobody was in sight.

So at this point, we were backtracking the country road to I-10 when we approached the 4-way stop sign and came to a stop. No other vehicles were in sight. I began to pull forward through the intersection when I spotted a flash of turquoise to my right. Out of nowhere, an old or vintage pickup truck was barreling towards us.

It all happened so fast! He was going to hit us. My husband tucked his head in his hands and then between his knees. At the same time, my son shouted out, "*He's not gonna stop!*" I realized we were not going to make it across the road and there wasn't enough room for the truck to get by us. I gritted my teeth and closed my eyes, waiting for the collision.

A few moments later, we opened our eyes and looked around. We had, in fact, made it across the intersection, but how? My husband looked down the road and saw that truck nearly half a mile down the road already. Did the truck go right through us?

"*What just happened?*" my husband asked.

We just sat there looking around and out the windows without an answer. That's when my son said, "*We better get going or we might be late.*"

"*That's enough for one day,*" I said while looking up to the Heavens. My husband agreed and commented that our Angels must have been looking over us.

We made it to camp on time, with a few minutes to spare. We enrolled our son and my husband and I just hung out in the gymnasium for a while.

"*So, have you figured out what happened back there?*" he asked.

"*No. Even that burger joint was weird.*"

"*Yeah.*"

The following morning, we both said goodbye and wished our son well before heading back to Houston.

On the way, we decided to stop at that Whataburger to see if we'd just lost our minds or something. I kid you not; we drove up and down that stretch of 2-lane road several times, but the Whataburger wasn't there! There were only a few farmhouses for about a mile, and not a business in sight - let alone a burger place. The intersection was there and we both double-checked to make sure we went the same direction this time. We did. It was like something out of the Twilight Zone.

During the return trip to Austin at the conclusion of football camp, we didn't bother taking the detour again. My son asked about it as we passed the turnoff. We couldn't tell him the restaurant wasn't there, just that we still haven't figured out what happened.

Chapter 13

My Friend Finally Saw It

Afternoon Close Encounter

A friend had once told me that he really wanted to see a Bigfoot. Then, maybe 2 or 3 years later, while headed into the neighboring town to do some shopping, we drove past a group of people stopped on the side of the highway. We weren't sure if they were all together or just random people pulled off the side of the road at the same time. It just seemed odd that so many people were gathered at the same time in that spot. The weather was maybe in the 70s with a clear blue sky, and if my memory serves me, it was probably 2:00 in the afternoon.

We both commented on the spectacle of seeing so many people and wondered what was happening. Nevertheless, we continued driving for another several miles to a small grocery store. There, we both got what we needed and then headed back home.

This time, as we approached the crowd, we pulled over. I told him I was going to take some photos of the beaver dam that was located off to the side. Fortunately, there wasn't anyone in that area, so I was free to take my time photographing the felled trees, flooding, and the beaver dam itself. My friend, however, walked right into the mess of people. Apparently, some were from a single family, while the others had just pulled over for a break and to stretch their legs.

We were probably there about 10 minutes when I thought to cross the river below the beaver dam and see what was in the woods. Something or someone told me not to, so I stopped halfway across the river and retreated back towards my vehicle.

That's when I saw my friend standing next to a woman on the river bank. He was pointing into the woods on the other side of the river. I didn't bother with the walk in their direction and decided to instead review my photos while waiting inside the Jeep.

After another 5-10 minutes, he returned, and we headed home.

Fast forward three whole years. He was visiting family in Florida, and I was still in my small mountain town. He called and said, *"There's something I need to tell you."*

His words were strange, as he's never said that before. I wondered what was to follow.

"Remember that day we pulled off to see what everyone was doing?" he asked.

"Yes," I replied.

"Well, while you were taking pictures of the beaver dam, I walked along the river bank while looking down into the river for potential fishing holes. Remember?"

"Yes."

"At one point, I looked up and across the river into the woods... and I think I saw a Bigfoot."

Now shocked, I said, *"What?"*

"*It was standing behind a tree and moving or swaying its upper body from side to side while watching me. When I realized it was staring at me and we made eye contact, I pulled my head down and looked away, thinking to myself, oh shit!*"

"*Wait. That was three years ago and you're just now telling me?*" I exclaimed.

"*Yeah. I didn't know what to say.*"

"*What else happened?*" I asked.

"*Well, after looking away for a moment, I lifted my head and looked back towards it. It had moved in just a brief second or two to my right, say 50 feet or more, and was shaking another tree. That tree looked to be about 12-14 inches in diameter. The whole tree was swaying as it rocked it with just its arms.*"

"*What do you mean, its arms?*"

"*It grabbed the tree and shook it. You know, without using its entire body to force the tree to move.*"

"*There was also a woman nearby that I called over to ask if she could see it too.*"

"*Right, I remember seeing her beside you as you pointed into the woods.*"

"*Yeah, that's when I asked her if she saw it.*"

"*What did she say?*" I asked.

"*Well, she just stood there for a moment, then asked me if that was my friend. Evidently, she saw us pull up and exit the Jeep, so she had seen you.*"

He continued, "*After I answered that you weren't 9 feet tall and all black, she paused for a second while trying to comprehend what she was seeing.*"

She finally asked, "*Is that a Bigfoot?*"

He turned towards her and said that he didn't know. When they looked back across the river, it was gone.

"I can't believe you didn't tell me about this for 3 years. Especially after saying you wanted to see one!"

"I know. I needed time, I guess, to think about what I really saw and if it really was a Sasquatch," he replied.

That's the end of his encounter, but I'd like to add something to his overall experience. Whenever he was in town visiting during the 3 years since having this experience and before telling me about it, he'd crash at my place. Before going to bed each night, I'd download several Bigfoot encounter stories from different YouTube channels and set them to play on my computer in the living room. Some of them were over an hour long and he'd listen to them while crashed on the couch. I can't say how many hours in all he consumed of other people's Bigfoot encounter stories, but I think they all helped him cope with the trauma of what shocked his beliefs that day.

Even after he returned to Florida, he continued to listen to people's stories, and that gave him the courage and confidence to tell me what he experienced that day. Though it was a non-threatening experience, it still shook him to his core and challenged his beliefs.

In the days, weeks, and months that followed, he searched his memories of any other times he may have experienced Bigfoot activity. Namely, while deer hunting on his family farm in Indiana.

This was prompted by many of the Bigfoot show call-ins he listened to by fellow hunters.

For example, he recalls the time he heard what he always thought was a smack on water by a beaver's tail, but now wonders if it was a tree knock/smack on a tree from Sasquatch. His mind told him it was probably just a beaver, even though he knew they didn't have beaver. Then there's the tree falling close to him while he was perched silently in his tree stand listening for deer. He said it was so loud and close; it sounded like a huge tree crashing to the ground. It really startled him, as he didn't hear anyone else out there with him and it was so sudden. When he was done hunting for the day, he climbed down the tree and went in search of the tree. To this day, he's never found it and that's confused him. Hearing other people call in to Bigfoot podcasts and YouTube shows to detail their strange run-ins with Bigfoot and/or Dogmen is helping to make sense of many memories he's had over the years while hunting.

Chapter 14

They Wanted Her

Mother Narrowly Avoids Abduction

O ne afternoon, a local researcher came into the store to share her time-lapse photos of strange craft photographed over the area in the early morning hours. We talked for about thirty minutes or more about the craft, ascension and trajectory, and possible viewing locations for future sightings before she hurried out the door for another meeting.

Just as she was closing the door, another woman, who was already inside and waiting to talk, was introduced to me.

She said triangle craft were gliding quietly into the area near her home nightly. As she was on her way out of town for a while, she wanted us to take the keys to her home and asked us to take as much time as we needed to document her reports.

When we looked up her home address online, we noticed right away that her home was in the general area of the flight path reported by the researcher, who had just left. We also found statements online regarding underground military installations nearby, in addition to the woman's claim that NASA was coming out the following week to investigate. Sounded like fun to us, so we loaded up our camping gear and hit the road the following afternoon.

When we arrived at her home, we noticed that it was situated on the side of a fairly steep hill, so pitching our tents was out of the question. The surrounding trees were also pretty tall and would most likely prevent decent camera footage of incoming craft, so we decided to head for another location about 15 minutes south of her home.

We arrived at the campgrounds about one hour before sunset and hurried to get everything set up before dark. Our one campsite was actually comprised of three adjacent sites, so we were able to spread out and set up various equipment in their own space so as not to get disturbed. It also allowed us to keep the equipment out and ready for when needed at a moment's notice.

Just after dinner and when it was dark enough, everyone gathered together in order to hike up the side of a nearby hill. When we found a small clearing, we all stopped and found a comfortable position to lie on our backs and look up into the night sky.

It was while in this location that I felt a presence just up the hill from our group. I wasn't the only one who picked up on this, as one of the two dogs also sensed it and became distracted. I didn't hear anything or see anything, however. It was more like sensing when someone is looking at you from a distance. Somehow, you just know when you're being watched.

I took the dog and walked about 50 feet further up the hillside, stopping where it felt like someone had just been. The dog looked around nervously and whimpered a few times. I looked around for a fallen tree and decided to sit down for a moment. Looking back toward the rest of the group, I tried to get a feeling of what it was like being quietly observed from this location. I comforted the dog by assuring her it was alright and a few moments later, we rejoined the group. All the while, I had the feeling someone or something had moved to a point just over the crest of the hill.

Fast-forwarding about 4 or 5 hours, the three girls resigned within their tent a few yards from the fire. Their tent was an open-sky model, meaning the roof of the tent was made of a screen fabric similar to the window covering in order to allow occupants to gaze at the stars from within the tent.

Around midnight, I was in my tent changing clothes when I heard the girls yell that a UFO was hovering directly over their tent and just above the trees. My tent also had an open-sky view, but I was further over in the first campsite and unable to see what they were talking about.

By the time I was out of my tent, the craft had moved away and out of sight, being blocked by the tall pine trees that surrounded us.

I asked the girls what happened. Evidently, a circular craft hovered briefly over their tent, as if waiting for them to spot it before leaving. Once they saw it and started yelling, the object began to move slowly to their left. This meant it was heading in the direction of the clearing everyone was at earlier to sky-watch. They described it as being a black circle craft with red and orange lights rotating around it, with a ring of white lights rotating in the opposite direction within the ring of red/orange lights.

None of us adults saw what the children described. For some strange reason, all of us adults were off in different locations and distracted by some task when this happened. For example, I was away from the group and inside my tent putting warmer clothes on. Others were putting things away for the evening and one person was setting up a telescope in our third camp site. When the girls saw the craft, everyone else was effectively disposed of in remote locations away from the girl's tent. The pine trees were so tall and thick that you couldn't see the sky above another campsite, even if it was the one next to your own.

The interesting thing about this whole incident was the direction in which the craft headed once the girls saw it. I hadn't told anyone about my experience of being watched up on the hillside, so it seemed more than coincidental that the craft headed back up the hill toward that spot.

A couple of hours later, the children were asleep and the rest of us were once again doing our own thing in various parts of our campsites. Two of us spent some time doing Astro-photography with a telescope. When finished, I returned to sit near the fire.

This was when I noticed the strange behavior from two of the others. They were talking about something and were very quiet about it. When I asked what was going on, I had no idea the answer was going to keep me up for several more hours.

The woman explained that while she was cleaning up dinner items and putting things away a little while earlier, she noticed a strange light. A beam of white light came from the hillside where we were earlier and stopped at her feet. When she looked down at her feet and at the light, she entered into a trance-like state and, without telling any of us, began following the light through the woods and up the hill.

As she walked through the woods, she knew she was going to enter a craft and that she would be okay. In fact, she said the light made her feel giddy and safe. Moving further and further up the hill, she said she knew what was about to happen and that she was going to board the craft. She wished the rest of us were with her and could join her in the contact and flight in the UFO.

This is when it dawned on her that she was alone. Her motherly instinct also kicked in, as she worried about who would take care of her daughter while she was away. At that moment, she said she yelled out my name, and the light disappeared. The trance was then broken, leaving her to wonder where she was and how to return to our campsite. Still feeling a little foggy, she decided to just head down the hill and look for a road and then our campsites.

It was at that point she informed her boyfriend of what happened and that's also when I arrived at the fire and noticed them talking quietly near their vehicle.

After sharing her incredible experience with me, I grabbed a flashlight, my camera, a set of the night vision goggles, and told her to show me where it happened. I wanted to see where the light was coming from. The two of us headed back up the hillside and in a matter of a minute or two, we had already lost visual sight of our camp.

Incredibly, she took me to the location where the dog and I sensed someone observing us. From there, we continued up the hill and to the left. As strange as this may sound, the trees appeared to form a hallway, and she confirmed that was where she was when she broke free of the trance and the light disappeared. We continued up the tree-lined hallway until it stopped, hoping to figure out where they were leading her.

Right there in front of us was another amazing sight. A strange circular clearing was made by cutting the trees, and this was located at the top of the hill. We have no idea when it was made or why it was made so far up the hill, but one thing was certain: that was at the end of the hallway of trees she was being led. In fact, she was almost at the end of that hallway when the light disappeared.

By the time we reached this clearing, there was no presence of a ship or beings like I observed hours earlier. I said, "*Whatever or whoever was here, they're gone now.*"

We snapped several photographs using the night-vision goggles and returned to tell the two other adults what we found. I returned in the morning for daylight photos and to get a better sense of the area.

The first thing I'd like to comment on is that once again, everyone in the group was distracted or were otherwise moved to different parts of the campsite to allow for her contact. This is common when a single person needs to be taken from a larger group of people.

The second point is that I find it curious that when this woman broke the trance and the light vanished, it was after she called out my name. While this might be nothing more than her intention to not continue, it's actually the second time she had contact with extraterrestrials and called out my name to end it when she became frightened.

Briefly, in the first instance, she was indoors with someone else and they were hiding behind a bed mattress. She told me they were coming for her and that she was going to be taken onto a craft. That's when she said to her visitors, "*Todd said I don't have to go.*"

This ended the encounter, and they were left behind. They've apparently come for her before.

During this camping incident, however, she decided against going onto the craft because she didn't want to leave her daughter behind. That's when she called out my name, as she knew it had stopped them previously.

Chapter 15

Invisible Friends

Child Finally Tells the Truth

Before leaving or while on the way to the first hot-spot, I like to ask tour guests why they signed up for the outing. In a room full of people, it's a great way to get to know each other and learn of potential issues which could arise.

In the case of a single family, the common response is that one of the adults, most often the father, is super into UFOs and Bigfoot.

In a few cases, fingers point to a child. This particular evening, fingers pointed to their 10-year-old son. He was big into aliens.

I asked him the usual questions, like *"Have you ever seen an alien?"* and *"Would you like to go on a UFO?"* and *"Are you excited to see something tonight?"*

Then it was time to get going.

Our first stop was roughly 20 miles away. When close, I asked the boy several more questions, but this time they weren't about UFOs or aliens.

While asking my questions, I kept an eye on his parents in the rear-view mirror for their reactions.

My first question was, *"Do you have any invisible friends?"*

The boy answered, "*Yes. I have one.*"
His parents looked at one another.

My second question was, "*Do you know his name?*"
The boy answered, "*His name is Ricardo.*"
Again, his parents looked at one another.

My third question was, "*Do you have any other invisible friends?*"
This is when he went silent.

His parents looked at him and waited for his answer, but they already knew something was wrong. He took too long to answer.

It took him almost 20 seconds to respond, finally saying, "*I do have other invisible friends, but my parents don't know about them.*"
His parents looked at one another, then back at their son.

My fourth and final question was, "*How many of them are there?*"
The boy answered, "*Nine.*"
Their jaws fell to the floor! His parents were speechless.

If my memory is correct, I didn't hear anyone speak again until we were out of the vehicle at our first stop.

Chapter 16

So Lin - So La Ra

This Mantra Brought Them

A ll she said was that a couple with direct contact experience was in possession of a chant or mantra used to call in extraterrestrials. In fact, the mantra was given to one of their friends living in South America by ETs while onboard their craft.

"*It's my day off and I'm at the store with a cart full of groceries,*" I told my boss.

"*Not only that, I'm about a half hour away.*"

"*That's okay. They know you're off, but still want you to take them out. I also want you to,*" she replied.

"*It's already past 8 o'clock and I'm not done getting what I need,*" I pleaded.

"*Todd, you have to do this for them. I'm going out with you guys too and they already told me they will wait until you get here.*"

We finally agreed to all meet at a location about halfway to our primary destination.

Standing at the trailhead on a popular hiking trail, they explained how they got the mantra and how successful it was at calling in ETs.

They said, *"While staying at our friend's home in Brazil, we had contact with more than one race of ETs."*

My boss and I listened as they continued.

"Her early ET abductions date all the way back to when she was a little girl. As you would expect, the visitations were scary and traumatic, but as she grew older, she thought of them more as friendly checkups."

"Over time, though, things took an unexpected turn for her. They began taking her young daughter and that terrified her all over again."

"Understanding her fear, during her next checkup, the ETs told her they wouldn't harm her daughter. They then gave her a mantra that, when repeated three times, would summon them so they could show her what they were doing and why."

Knowing a little more about where it came from, we all agreed to repeat the mantra three times and see for ourselves.

As far as we could tell, nothing happened, so we tried it again. Still nothing. Well, we felt something, but that was common in the area we were in.

What we felt was what many hikers experience – hearing invisible people walking around us. The invisibles were likely curious.

Wondering if we did something wrong, I asked, *"How long after saying it did it take for the ETs to show up?"* and also, *"Has it ever worked for you two, you know, since you returned home?"*

"No, it hasn't," she said.

He added, *"It's only worked when our friend was present and leading the mantra."*

"We hoped that coming back for another outing with you, that it might work," the woman continued.

"As for how long it took for them to arrive," the husband answered, *"it wasn't right away."*

"Because there were so many people at her home that night, they didn't appear in the middle of the living room like we half expected."

His wife continued, *"Yeah, it was like they waited for us to all go to bed. Afterwards, they visited each of us, or one room at a time. Some people only saw lights, some actually saw the beings."*

"For example," she continued, *"after we were in our bedroom and in bed, we noticed a dazzling light appear from under the door. We learned the next morning that the people sleeping in the living room experienced a visit by round balls of light."*

"We also heard from others that they too had experiences once in bed," the man added.

This all sounded convincing enough, so I suggested we try repeating the mantra at a couple more locations. They agreed, but again, nothing happened.

Our evening was uneventful.

After dropping them off and on my long drive home, I continued to reflect on the evening's activities and, a few times, recited the mantra repeatedly. Still nothing. I'm sure they did too on their way home.

I even opened my car's moon roof and looked up at the stars once I was outside of town and didn't have the interference of light pollution.

"Were they up there following me?" I wondered to myself. Nope. Nothing.

I believed their story and wondered what the reason was for a lack of response. After all, I've had face-to-face encounters of my own, so I believed using a mantra like this was possible.

I would soon figure it out.

Lying in bed that evening, I repeated the mantra until I felt it was time to shut down and get some sleep. I had some pretty interesting dreams, but none included contact.

The following evening, I couldn't sleep. I'd been working late again and tossed and turned all night long, as my mind continued to work.

Around 1:30 AM. I was laying in bed with my eyes closed and said the mantra a few more times. I remember thinking to myself, "*I REALLY wish they would come.*"

As I thought this, I had the sense that my heart stirred or that the intent was coming from my heart. It was more than simple words coming out of my mouth. I desired their presence with all of my heart.

In the instant I completed the thought, I heard and felt an electric buzzing or vibrating sound around me and then realized I couldn't move.

I opened my eyes and noticed a dull silver-white light or ball of energy of some sort spinning in place about four feet off the floor, a few feet from my bed.

"*They finally heard me and came to visit,*" I thought to myself.

Excited, I continued to watch the light spin in place. Then I got the feeling someone was about to materialize right in front of me, and not a moment later, that's exactly what happened!

The humanoid being was maybe 6 feet tall, though I can't be sure. I still couldn't move and in the dark bedroom, I could only see so much.

Lying on my stomach, my head was flat on the mattress, which also limited my vision from around his knees upwards. He appeared to be wearing a dark brown robe with the hood draped over his head.

Once he materialized in the middle of my bedroom, he quickly took a step towards me while reaching out to me. As he did so, I said *"Thank you"* in my thoughts, for I was grateful for his visit.

I wanted to get up and talk with him, so I struggled with all my might to push myself up against the electric paralysis. As I did so, I briefly looked away from him and down at my bed. When I looked back up at him, he was gone and so was the paralysis.

I jumped out of bed and looked outside my window to see if I could see if anything was above the house. Nothing.

"Where did he go?"

It made little sense. Why would they go through all the trouble of teleporting into my room to only disappear before I could meet them? Wasn't that understood by my struggles to get the mantra right?

It would be several years later before I realized what really happened that night: He took me with him.

Why did it take me so long to see it? I don't know. Maybe it has something to do with how we notice things happening to others, but not ourselves.

In the exact moment when I was struggling to get up out of bed against the paralysis, he touched me. When he did, he took me somewhere. I have no memory of it. Then, when they sent me back, it was again in the exact moment when I was pushing myself up to talk with him. That's also when the paralysis left and I could move. I sat up and he was gone.

Actually, he didn't come back with me. You could say they beamed me back to the same moment they took me. Everything that took place between those moments is a blank, and I'm not sure how long I was gone.

The next day, I told the store owner what happened. He didn't believe me and laughed, "*Yeah, right!*"

With all the strange things we'd been through guiding tours and sky-watches for other people, his disbelief seemed a little odd.

While talking to a friend about what happened, I recalled a conversation with a woman who came into the shop once to share her stories of abductions.

She said that each time they came for her, she first felt the same electric buzzing sensation and paralysis. Then they showed themselves or entered the room she was in.

They approached her only after she couldn't move, also touching her to beam aboard their craft. After about four visitations, she said she finally settled down and was no longer scared.

She told me, "*I thought, okay, they're back and went with it. Every time they came, it was the same.*"

In her case, and like the South American mother in this story, she transitioned over time from being a victim or someone taken against her will, to being a contactee, no longer afraid, and went willingly.

Chapter 17

They Abandoned Everything

Wood Cutters vs Sasquatch

I was talking with a restaurant owner about some of the Bigfoot stories people had shared with me.

The first story was about a woman living near the Colorado/New Mexico border. She told me that she often catches the Sasquatch looking in the windows of her house and that they often leave tracks all over her property.

One time, when her visiting sister was returning to the house from her car, she noticed a large brown-haired Sasquatch walking up the mountain behind the house.

As you can imagine, the restaurant owner didn't believe a word I said.

It would turn out the following morning a customer came in and sat down for breakfast.

She greeted him and asked where he was from.

His answer was the exact same town from my story.

"Really?" she asked.

"*Have you ever seen a Bigfoot?*"

The man turned completely pale and said, "*Well, yes. That's why I'm here right now.*"

He continued, "*A couple days ago, a team of guys and I were cutting fuel wood in a permit area, when a large rock suddenly landed between myself and the other men.*"

"*I looked at the rock and then up at the men. They were frozen with fear and staring at the tree line behind me. I turned to see what they were looking at.*"

"*There, standing in the open about 40 yards away, was a large Sasquatch, around 7–8 feet tall.*"

"*We all dropped our gear and raced down the mountain in our trucks.*"

He added that all their equipment was still up there and that he was trying to figure out how to retrieve it over breakfast, as none of the other men wanted to go back with him.

Chapter 18

Children of the Woods

They Like Our Toys & Soda Pop

One evening, my friend Tammy and her family were quietly at home preparing for bed, when her and her husband Jim heard a ruckus coming from the garbage dumpster down the hill at the end of their driveway. It's one of those big brown dumpsters that belongs to the county and is where they and their two neighbors place their garbage for pickup every two weeks. The ruckus coming from the dumpster sounded like a bear was trying to get inside for a late-night snack.

Tammy looked over at Jim and asked if he'd locked the dumpster lids after taking the garbage out earlier that day. This is common practice when you live in the mountains during the spring and summer months. Jim said he did, so they both shrugged their shoulders and figured the bear would move on to another dumpster when it couldn't get inside theirs. This has happened many times before whenever they forget to lock the lids or before they hear that the bears are out of hibernation. However, they soon heard more loud thumps and bangs. Then there was the unmistakable slow screech from the rusty hinges. The bear just managed to open the lock and lifted the lid to get inside!

"*Crap!*" yelled Tammy as they both jumped to their feet.

Jim reached for the flashlight while Tammy switched on the front porch light and before they both stepped outside onto their porch. Using the beam from the flashlight, they could both see the large hungry bear with black fur digging around inside the dumpster.

"*So you locked the dumpster, huh?*" she said.

Jim huffed and just looked back at her, "*Yes, I did*," while rolling his eyes.

BANG! That was the second lip falling backwards against the top of the dumpster.

When they returned their gaze upon the bear, they could tell it was still digging around inside the container, but something wasn't right. The bear didn't jump inside or climb up on top of the bin like they usually do.

"*What is that laying on the ground next to the dumpster?*" Tammy asked.

Jim squinted his eyes a bit to better his focus in the low light.

"*It looks like a couple of trash bags. Those look like the trash bags I took out earlier today!*" he concluded.

They looked at each other with a puzzled look on their faces, as the bear appeared to be shuffling the trash around. Jim didn't want to clean up the expected mess, so he yelled at the bear to go away.

"*Yah! Hey Bear! Yah!*"

Then the ruckus stopped, and the bear lowered the lid and stood up straight, looking back at them.

"Oh, crap!" said Tammy, "*That's a Bigfoot!*"

They've heard about several sightings before, but those happened 10-15 miles away. This was too close, and it shocked them. They didn't know Sasquatches came around people's homes like this.

As the 8-9 foot tall Sasquatch stared back at them, all Jim could say was, *"Sorry to bother you. We'll go back inside now and let you continue with your business."*

Jim turned and looked at Tammy, then motioned her to come inside with him. Once back in the living room, Tammy reached back for the light switch out of habit, then as she was about to turn off the porch light, she thought it best to leave it on to give their unusual neighbor some light in case they needed it.

Jim and Tammy stayed up talking about the incident for about 30 more minutes before turning in. The kids were still in their bedrooms and didn't hear any of what had just transpired. Their bedrooms were on the back side of the house, so they didn't see the porch light come on or the visiting Sasquatch. Tammy and Jim agreed not to say anything to the children, but would tell them not to stay out after dark just to be safe.

In the morning, Tammy was the first to get up and, after turning on the coffeemaker, put her slippers on and quietly walked outside and to the end of their driveway. The previous night's events were weighing heavily on her mind. As she made her way closer and closer to the dumpster, she noticed the garbage bags were nowhere in sight. She was sure they would have a mess to clean up, with the ravens and other critters looking for a morning feast.

"Where are the garbage bags? Did the Sasquatch take them with him?" she wondered.

She reached the end of the driveway and turned to the left to approach the two-lid dumpster.

"*Oh my God,*" she said softly to herself.

Standing motionless about six feet from the dumpster, Tammy just stared at the locks and tried to make sense of what she was looking at.

"*The locks are secured in place on both lids…*" she mumbled aloud.

By this time, Jim had seen her from inside the living room and went out to join her. She hadn't heard him approaching, but his presence next to her jarred her out of deep thought.

"*Was the whole thing just a dream of some sort?*" she asked.

Unsure what she meant, he asked what she was talking about.

Tammy lifted her right arm and pointed at the locked lids before looking back at him.

He was quiet for a moment, then said, "*See, I told you I locked the dumpster!*"

Jim let out a chuckle and walked over to the dumpster to unlock the lids.

"*I wonder what it was looking for,*" Tammy said. "*If it was a bear, it was looking for food. But it wasn't a bear. So was it also looking for food?*"

Looking inside the dumpster, Jim said, "*Everything looks normal. No bags are torn apart and the two kitchen bags I put in here yesterday are right where I put them.*"

"*What do you mean, Jim? That Sasquatch put them back inside the dumpster, then locked the lids and left?*" She was confused. "*Would a Bigfoot really do that?*"

Jim didn't answer. He didn't know the answer and was curious. "*What was the Bigfoot looking for if not food scraps?*"

"*I don't know,*" she said. "*Maybe the neighbors saw the bags beside the dumpster this morning and put them inside so the birds wouldn't get at them and make a mess.*"

It sounded logical. But then Jim noticed something.

"*Wait a minute,*" he said, as he pulled the garbage bags out one by one and placed them on the ground. He continued to remove everything until he could see to the bottom of the bin. Something was missing.

"*Tammy, come look at this,*" he said as he motioned to her while pointing inside the dumpster. She looked inside and didn't see anything unusual, but then it clicked.

"*The broken rocking horse is missing!*" she exclaimed. "*Do you think it took it, or maybe one of the neighbors saw it and took it?*"

"*I don't know, maybe they did,*" Jim wondered.

Then he continued, "*But if they didn't and the Sasquatch took it, do you think it knew it was here and came for it once it got late and we were getting ready for bed?*" That was a loaded question, and he knew it.

Tammy replied, "*That would mean it was watching us, right? But from where? And what would that huge Bigfoot want with a toddler's broken rocking horse?*"

Then it made sense. Whether or not it knew the rocking horse was there didn't really matter. They could simply ask the neighbors if they pulled it from the garbage.

Jim replied, "*What was important was that it may have been the father of a young Sasquatch and that there could be a family of them nearby.*"

While they discussed the matter, their two kids had gotten out of bed and noticed the house was empty. Looking around for their parents, they spotted them outside at the road. They both put on shoes and walked out to join their parents.

Billy, their 12-year-old son, asked, "*What's going on and why is the trash piled up in the yard?*"

Jim and Tammy just looked at each other. They weren't prepared to discuss what had happened the night before, and they still didn't know what to say. After all, what were they doing at the dumpster with a big pile of garbage laying at their feet? What did the neighbors think?

Tammy looked at her husband and said, "*Just tell them. They're old enough.*"

"*Old enough for what?*" their daughter Sarah chimed in.

"*Last night, after you two went to bed, we had a visitor. He, or it, was going through our garbage, but didn't make a mess or dig through the garbage bags.*"

Their dad continued, "*Your mother and I thought it was just another bear, but it managed to unlock the lids and when we yelled at it, it stood up and looked at us. It wasn't a bear.*"

Billy asked, "*What was it?*"

"*It looked like a Bigfoot,*" his dad continued. "*We left it alone and went to bed. This morning, your mother and I came out to see what it may have been looking for or what it took out.*"

Their mother added, "*We both agree that for the time being, we want both of you to be inside the house by the time it gets dark. No playing outside after dark until we know more, okay?*"

"*Okay,*" Billy and Sarah said at the same time.

The day went on as normal as possible. The kids played with friends for most of the afternoon before returning home for dinner. When Jim returned from work, they all sat at the dinner table and quietly ate.

"*Dad?*" Billy asked.

"Yes son?"

"I was thinking about what you said this morning. Did you find out what the Bigfoot took or what it was looking for?"

"No. Your mother and I thought it was food, but it didn't open any bags or take the garbage. At least not that we can tell. We did notice your sister's old rocking horse was missing, though."

Sarah sat up straight. *"What?"*

"I'd thrown the rocking horse away recently, as a leg was broken and you're eight now and no longer play with it," he replied.

Sarah looked at her mom with a pouting expression, as if waiting for her mom to say something.

But it was Billy who spoke next.

"Why would a Bigfoot take a human toy?"

"Your mother and I think it may have children of its own, or maybe the neighbors or someone else took it with plans to repair it."

"Bigfoot children?" Billy repeated out loud, looking at his little sister. *"Do you think they like toys like we do?"*

Sarah added, *"Do you think their children play at human playgrounds?"*

Tammy jumped in and added that it could be possible, but there's no telling. *"Besides,"* she concluded, *"we really don't know if the Bigfoot took your rocking horse. Until we do, just keep your eyes open when you guys play outside or with your friends. We still want you two in by dark and no going out after dinner!"*

Life returned to normal, with no more visible bear or Sasquatch activity. That is, until we had our first good snow. It was early November and temperatures dropped enough to allow for about a foot of fresh snow.

The following afternoon, Billy came running home, wet from snow, all out of breath and barely able to talk. He said he was out in the canyon checking on his trap lines after the snow stopped, when something strange happened! While walking across a meadow to locate the first game trail in the trees on the opposite side, small branches and sticks started landing in the snow in front of him. He stopped and looked to see who it was, but nobody was out there with him. In fact, his footprints in the snow were the only tracks he could see.

"*When I started walking towards the woods, the sticks appeared to land in the snow again and again, but nobody was there. Mom, I swear it's the truth.*"

"*Maybe it was the wind,*" Sarah said with a smirk.

"*But there's more,*" Billy continued.

"*I started running to the trees and then I stopped after I entered the woods. The flying branches had stopped, so I just stood there looking around and listening.*"

"*Listening for what?*" his younger sister asked.

"*I wanted to see if someone was out there with me. Then I heard them.*"

"*Them?*" his mother asked with one raised eyebrow.

"*Yes. I'm telling you guys the truth and I'm not kidding. I heard kids giggling!*"

"*What would kids be doing way out there in the woods after that snow?*" Tammy asked.

"*I don't know, but I know what I heard!*"

Then Billy quietly asked his mom, "*Do you think it could have been that Bigfoot's children?*"

"*What? Let's stop talking about this, and just wait until your father gets home from work. We'll talk more about it then.*"

"*Okay,*" as he turned and went to his room. He glanced over at his sister and she just shook her head.

Both kids were in their rooms when Jim got home from work. Tammy pulled him aside before he went any further, to tell him what happened to Billy.

"*What should we do?*" Tammy asked him.

"*Let me get cleaned up and we can talk afterwards. I really need a hot shower right now.*"

Tammy went back into the kitchen and started warming up dinner. She called the kids to help set the table and get cleaned up. She stopped Billy and told him his father was taking a shower and that he could talk about his encounter during dinner, but only if his father asked him about it.

"*Your father had a long day and wants to unwind, so you should be respectful of your father's wishes.*"

"*Alright mom,*" Billy said as he continued setting plates on the table.

That evening, the dinner-table discussion turned out to be more interesting than anyone could have expected.

After Billy shared what happened with his father, Jim sat there quietly and said nothing for about five minutes. The kids just looked at him and then over at their mom. Billy remembered to respect his dad and that he had a long day. Everyone just waited for him to look up from his plate and say something.

Tammy reached over and touched Jim's arm, asking, "*Is everything okay?*"

He looked up and then at her. Then he looked at the kids across the table from him.

"*What's wrong dad,*" asked Sarah.

He smiled and said, "*Everything's fine, honey. Daddy just had a long day.*"

Billy spoke up and asked what he thought of his experience in the meadow earlier and who he thought might have thrown those branches.

Jim turned to look at Tammy and gave a sigh.

"*I have something to tell all of you, but I don't know how to begin. I suppose I should start with Billy and what happened this afternoon, but I think I'll start with what happened to me this morning.*"

"*What happened, dad?*" asked Billy.

"*This morning on my way to work, it was still dark out and I had my brights ongoing through the canyon. Before the turnoff, I noticed something large standing on the side of the road and just at the edge of my lights. As I slowed for the turn, it stepped out into the road so I could see it.*"

"*What was it daddy?*" Sarah interrupted.

"*It stood on two legs like the Bigfoot that visited us last summer, but it was reddish brown. Not black like the one that picked through our garbage. It was also a female.*"

Jim looked back at Tammy with a blank gaze and took a few deep breaths and collect his thoughts.

"*Honey, when I came home and you told me what happened to Billy, my mind started spinning. In the shower, I hoped the steam and hot water would help to clear my mind, but it didn't.*"

"*What do you mean, Jim?*" she asked.

After a long pause and a drink from his glass of water, he continued.

"*The Sasquatch walking out in the road ahead of me wasn't the only strange thing that happened this morning. I don't understand what's happening or why. Maybe there's some logical explanation. I just don't know."*

Jim slowly continued, "*After the morning shift change, the night crew packed up and went home. I was all alone in the office. One of the guys left an unopened can of Dr Pepper out on the counter and I put it outside on the cement post near the door. I figured it would be cold in about 30 minutes. After my morning checks, I opened the door and reached for the soda, but it was gone. I walked around in the dark and frigged cold looking for the can of pop, but I couldn't find it. As I scratched my head and turned to go back inside, I thought I heard giggling, like that of children."*

Chapter 19

Shots Fired

A Camper's Night of Terror

W hile at a local restaurant for dinner with friends, a woman approached my table.

The hostess was a friend and knew people had been sharing their Bigfoot stories with me.

She introduced me to a woman who had a story I might like to hear. Her story went like this:

> A man pulled his travel trailer up to one of the area's lakes for a few days of camping and fishing.

> It was raining and as he lay in bed trying to go to sleep, sudden screams and howls broke out from the surrounding hills.

He did not know what was making the noises, and they persisted to keep him awake. Frustrated, he got up and went outside to fire off a few rounds from his gun.

Silence. He returned to his bunk and, as he was about to doze off, something violently rocked and shook his camper from side to side. This continued to keep him awake until he passed out from fear and exhaustion.

When he awoke, the sun was up, and the rain had stopped. So too did the harassment.

He cautiously exited the camper and walked around his rig, looking for damage. There was none, but he saw some very large 17-inch footprints in the wet soil all around his trailer.

It wasn't a dream after all. It really happened. This terrified him. He packed up and hauled butt back down the mountain.

I don't know how this woman learned of his encounter, but suspect the man lived in the area as not too many outsiders know how to get there.

He may have shared his experience with someone she knew.

After she told me this story, I asked when it took place.

She said, "*A couple of weeks earlier.*"

That was interesting to me, as I was up at the lake the same day or the day before this man arrived.

A friend and I had visited the lake to photograph it from the air with a drone. As we got out of the car and started looking for a good place to launch the drone, I got the distinct feeling "*they*" were in the area.

From the sound of the man's story, they were.

Chapter 20

Halloween

"Oh Hell No!"

I t was a cold Halloween evening in the desert. Two gentlemen had just traveled halfway across the country to join me on an outing they'd hopefully never forget. In the end, it would be a life-changing evening for both of them.

They were both in their mid-twenties and were lifelong friends. Though they had grown up and done everything together, only one of them was a *"Believer."* Because of their strong friendship, I didn't understand how their beliefs about aliens and Bigfoot could be so different. You know, as our beliefs are largely determined from our experiences and environment, so with that always being the same with them, you could call me surprised.

It was 9 PM and our destination was about 20 miles into the middle of the desert, so we climbed into my vehicle and set off through town.

During the drive, I asked them both questions to help me get to know them a bit better. Mostly, I was curious about why the skeptic agreed to the expense of flying across the country on his buddy's quest into the unknown. I never really got a straight answer, so I left it at that. I did learn that it took a LOT of convincing for the skeptic to come along with us that night.

The moon was full and bright, lighting up the driveway in front of us.

"*Okay, we're here,*" I said.

My two guests opened their doors and looked around outside.

"*So, this is the famous ranch?*" asked the skeptic.

"*Yep,*" I replied. "*It's been abandoned for many years now.*"

I was at the back of the truck, going through bins of equipment for items we'd need. I called them over and handed them warm winter jackets.

"*Put these on. It's only going to get colder tonight.*"

I also handed each of them a couple of granola bars and a bottle of water, as well as a flashlight.

"*Okay, are you guys ready?*" I asked.

They both nodded their heads.

I proceeded to lead them up the dirt road to an old locked gate baring '*No Trespassing*' signs, where I gave them a lay of the land and go over what I had planned for them.

"*Before I lead you to the back of the property, I want to share some stories with you.*"

"*Take this gate, for instance. It's always locked. One evening, a young couple noticed from a distance it appeared to be unlocked. As they approached to get a better look, the gate mysteriously opened wide, as if inviting them in. During another visit, a man rested up against it while the group he was with talked. Suddenly, he was thrown back away from the gate as if someone had pushed the gate with tremendous force from the other side. Understandably, he didn't go near the gate again!*"

Both men stepped back away from the gate and looked it over. I'm sure they were wondering if I was trying to pull their leg.

"*It's also not uncommon to hear footsteps approaching the gate from the other side, but you cannot see anyone,*" I added. "*We've also had those invisible people out here walking around our groups and vehicles.*"

Just then, all three of us felt a cold chill as the wind picked up. We zipped our coats up even higher and they commented on how they were glad to have the jackets. They never thought it got so cold in the desert.

The believer asked, "*Is there something special we need to do to make contact? I mean, I've been asking in my thoughts for a sign or something, that they're here with us, but I'm not getting an answer. I believe something will happen, but I'm not picking up on anything.*"

"*I know most people feel seeing is believing, and therefore they always want to see a sign, but I suggest you not rely only on the sense of vision. Instead, be open to your other senses, like touch, smell, and hearing.*"

For the next 10-minutes, they asked about all the things they'd heard about the ranch and if they really happened. As I pointed out where each of those events took place, an unexpected feeling came over me.

"*Do you guys feel that?*" I asked.

"*What do you mean?*"

"*Well, are you still cold or do you feel like it's suddenly 70-degrees?*" They laughed, "*Yeah, you're right.*"

I laughed with them and the three of us unzipped our heavy jackets. It was no longer in the thirties and we welcomed the change.

"*There's something else happening,*" I added. "*Do you feel comfortable, like we could stand here talking all night and you don't need to sit down or go to the bathroom?*"

"*Yeah*," said the believer. "*My legs aren't feeling so stiff and my back feels relaxed.*"

"*Mine too*," added his friend.

At that point, I said, "*Stay here for a minute.*"

They watched as I walked slowly back up the road toward the vehicle, then stopped, took a few steps backward, then a few steps forward, a few steps back, and then extended my arm out in front of me.

When I returned, I said, "*I'll explain in a minute, but first, I want each of you to, one at a time, do what I just did. Walk slowly, being very aware of the temperature, the silence, and that there is currently zero wind blowing on us. As you walk, do so until you feel the wind and cold. Then, step backwards out of that cold and then forward into the cold.*"

They looked at each other and then at me as if I were crazy.

Smiling, I said, "*Trust me.*"

The believer went first. His friend and I stayed at the gate and watched as he did as instructed. He came back smiling. I put my finger up to my lips as if asking him to not say anything.

"*Okay, it's your turn*," I said to the skeptic.

He walked past his friend and ended up stopping at the same point as us, some 30 feet away.

"*What is this?*" he asked.

I pointed up at the sky and asked them if they could see any airplanes flying overhead or any satellites?

"*Can you hear anything, such as wind, insects, or coyotes?*" I asked them.

They both said no and asked what that meant.

I answered with a question. "*Have you heard of people that had Bigfoot encounters saying that everything around them went suddenly quiet first?*"

"*Yes,*" they both answered.

"*Well,*" I replied, "*That's what is happening right now, only you're noticing more of the finer details.*"

I continued, "*For example, when some people report the strange and sudden silence, it's often followed up with an equally sudden but terrifying scream or crash of a tree or rock, forcing them to quickly leave the area. They may even see the creature. At that moment in their life, they're only concerned with their safety and don't really pay attention to the finer details like you just experienced. Neither of you are in that flight or fight mode.*"

"*This phenomenon happens so often out here, you might even expect it,*" I said.

"*Has it really happened to you before?*" asked the skeptic.

"*Yes, many times, in fact.*"

I continued, "*However, the details vary. For instance, it's typically reported as a prelude to a Bigfoot encounter, but I've had it happen during other activities. Not just with Bigfoot.*"

"*While people report the sudden silence - as if the wind and all living things in the forest collude to go quiet at the same time - my experience has been that it's more like a giant invisible bubble which descends upon us and within that bubble, reality can be different for the people inside it.*"

"*What do you mean, exactly?*" asked the believer.

"*It's hard to explain, but you both have just experienced what I did, that you walked over there and found the edge of something. Here within the something, it is currently warm and comfortable. Outside the invisible something we all felt the same cold and wind, right?*"

They nodded in agreement.

"*Think about this for a moment,*" I added. "*If the forest goes silent during a Bigfoot encounter, how far does that silence extend? I mean, does it go out over the entire planet, or to the nearest city and why is that? It's like one of those things people don't think about.*"

I continued, "*So, what if all of that activity happens under a sort of invisible dome or bubble so that only those who are supposed to experience it do?*" I asked them. "*It's like we had this experience here at the gate and people over at the vehicle didn't. How is that?*"

Just then, the invisible '*something*' which had descended over us began to lift and the cold wind returned. We all felt it, and looking up, we could once more see airplanes flying overhead and we heard coyotes yipping in the distance.

"*See what I mean?*" I asked them. "*Do you believe that warmth and comfort we just experienced was felt by everyone in town or just us? And, I bet people in town could see and hear those airplanes overhead while standing here under this invisible 'something' we couldn't. That is, until it lifted.*"

"*I guess it makes sense that it was just over us,*" said the believer, "*as it was like it came and went.*"

The skeptic added, "*And we found the edge of it over there.*"

"*Exactly,*" I replied. "*The people who used to live here once said that while out in the yard behind the house, one person saw two dinosaurs back there by the trees and when she yelled to the other person who was standing about 20 feet away, they didn't hear her yelling their name or see anything unusual. The bubbles can be as small or large as needed.*"

"*I've even felt the edge of something like this much larger around a city, where I drove through it to get inside as it were, from the north, and again while leaving town to the west,"* I added. *"But that story's for another time. We've got more to do tonight,"* I told them.

"Let's head around back," I said, while illuminating the trail.

About 5 minutes later, we crested the top of the hill, which allowed us a view of the abandoned home. Before we reached the backyard, we were stopped in our tracks by the sound of something very large stomping on the ground, grunting, and breaking branches in the trees ahead of us. It was almost like something large was stuck in the trees and was trying to get out. Adding to the strangeness, not one of the trees moved or swayed with all that racket taking place.

"This is turning out to be a fun Halloween for you guys, huh?" I asked.

"What is it?" asked the skeptic.

"Let's wait and see if it makes its way out into the open," I replied.

Normally, we wouldn't be able to see much at night, even from the elevation of the hill, but the moon was full and lit up the entire desert below.

The crashing and branch snapping sounds continued for about a minute and then stopped. That's when the three of us hiked down the hill and toward the grove of trees. As we walked around to the back side, we could tell that was where the sounds had originated, but nothing was there. In fact, there were no broken branches or tree limbs on the ground anywhere!

"So what just happened?" asked the believer.

"The only thing I can think of is that a Sasquatch might have been back here."

"Why do you say that?" asked the friend.

"Well, this property has had Bigfoot activity, as reported by the former homeowner. In fact, she reported that her very first encounter happened

in a similar manner, but I don't know where on the ranch it took place. Before that, she didn't know she had Bigfoot hanging around."

I continued, *"She said that she heard loud sounds from branches being broken, stomping sounds, etc. just like what happened here with us. She would later have many encounters with a female Sasquatch, so she naturally made the connection."*

"I will add that I've brought people out here before and when talking about the area's female Sasquatch, we received vocalizations and other noises from various parts of the ranch. Once we heard noises coming from the parking area where we parked. When we returned to the vehicle, we did look for footprints, but didn't find any."

The three of us stayed a bit longer just talking and looking around before heading back to the locked gate. That's when things really took a turn for the paranormal.

I heard one of the guys unexpectedly say, *"I have this compelling urge to climb over the gate and go up to the house."*

When I turned to see who said it, it was the non-believer, the skeptic.

"What?" I responded.

"Yeah, I can't explain it. It's a really strong feeling that I can't shake," he reiterated.

His friend, the believer, asked, *"What do you mean, a feeling you can't shake?"*

"It's like I'm being called or beckoned to the house," he answered.

We watched as the man made his way up the drive to the house. We both remained silent and turned our hearing sensitivity to the maximum in case we needed to go after him.

I couldn't help but recall all the instances where someone or something made it very clear they didn't want people on *their* side of the fence. The simple fact he was allowed to make it to the house was curious, to say the least. Neither his friend nor I appeared to have been invited in.

A few minutes later, he returned, and we moved away from the gate and back to the vehicle.

"*So, what happened? Did you see anything?*" asked his friend.

"*Yeah, what happened?*" I added.

"*Well, all the way up to the house I continued to feel the strong need to keep going and that I would be alright. When I reached the front of the house and was about to step up onto the porch, I heard noises coming from inside the house.*"

"*What sort of noises?*" his friend asked.

"*It sounded like something fell over onto the floor and then I heard someone running away from the window. It was like someone was inside and watched me approach the house. As soon as I moved toward the porch like I was going to go in, they ran away to hide.*"

That's when I asked, "*Did the running sound like an animal or human, like an adult or child?*"

"*It wasn't very loud and was like quick, short steps, so maybe a child. It was definitely on two feet.*"

"*Did you go inside?*" asked his friend.

"*No. Something said I'd gone far enough, but I did look inside the window.*"

"*What did you see?*" I asked.

"*It was dark, but I could make out a kind of bar like in a saloon with pop bottles on it as well as toy cars on the floor under the window.*"

"*Do you still feel anything, like that urge to go to the house?*" his friend asked.

"*No. It's gone.*"

Before we packed up, I asked them both a question.

"*You guys seem to know a lot about the ranch. Have you ever heard the story about the boy with a scooter?*"

They both shook their heads. "*What is it?*" asked the believer.

"*I'll tell you, then we'll drive back home. It's already pretty late.*"

"*As the story goes, two guys drove out here during the day. About a mile from the house, they noticed a young boy walking alongside the road. He was carrying a scooter.*"

"*The guys in the car thought it weird, as they were in the desert and at least 20 miles from any paved surface, so where could he be going with a scooter?*"

"*When they pulled up to the boy, they asked if he was okay or needed a ride. The boy said yes, he was fine and that his scooter was broken, so he would like a ride.*"

"*Where are you going?*"

"*Up to the house,*" as he pointed in the direction they were headed.

"*This made their hair stand up, as they knew nobody lived there and all the stories they ever heard about the place were strange and paranormal. They were also curious, so they opened the door and let the boy in.*"

"*They stopped at the same locked gate and asked the boy if that was where he was going. He said yes and got out. He looked back at the guys and invited them up to the house for some soda pop and to play with cars. That was too much for them, so they declined and let the boy go.*"

"*They watched in silence as he crawled under the gate and made his way up to the house.*"

I continued, "*It's interesting that you saw pop bottles on the counter and also toy cars, not to mention hearing what sounded like a child running through the house.*"

They both looked at me in disbelief. "*You're kidding, right?*" asked the believer.

"*Nope. That's a report two guys made of their experience, so unless they lied, it could be true.*"

"*Let's get out of here,*" I added. "*It's already midnight and I'm cold.*"

Now, at this point, you might think this was all a bit much and probably not true. I assure you, this all happened, as well as what I'm about to conclude with. The events of their evening didn't end there.

While at work about a month later, I got a call from the skeptic guy. He was upset and wanted me to tell him what happened to his friend.

I had no idea what he was talking about.

"*He hasn't come home!*" he told me. "*We were supposed to fly back on the same flight, but after that night at the ranch, he told me he wanted to extend his stay a bit longer and that he'd fly home later.*"

Then he dropped a bombshell. "*Did he tell you what happened after we got back to the hotel that night?*"

"No," I answered. "*I haven't seen or heard from him since I dropped you guys off. What happened?*"

"*We returned to our hotel room and were getting into bed while remarking about some of the stuff that happened at the ranch.*"

"*I was in my bed, which was closest to the window, and he was in his, next to the bathroom. Suddenly, we both heard what sounded like some sort of humming ship descend and stop just outside the window by my bed.*"

He paused for a moment, then told me, "*I was terrified and there was no way in hell I wanted to see what was going to happen. I wanted no part of it!*"

He was still obviously still upset about it.

"So, what happened then?" I asked.

"I put my head under the blanket and refused to look, saying out loud, oh hell no!"

"Then in the morning, my friend told me two beings from the craft floated across the room to visit with him. It was then he decided to stay behind."

That's when he asked me again, *"So what the hell happened? He seemed different in some way and I got the feeling that we could no longer be friends."*

"I really have no idea! Have you heard from him? Has he called?"

"No. The last thing he said was that he wanted to stay behind for a while longer to explore his spiritual journey and would return home in a couple of weeks, but he hasn't returned."

I really didn't know what to say, other than assure him that if I saw his friend or heard from him, I'd be sure to have him call home.

I never did see him again, and that was also the last I'd heard from his friend.

Chapter 21

Anna's Stories

UFOs and Grey Aliens

As 14-year-old Anna sneaked out of the house and made her way to her favorite place, the tree swing sat atop the hill, motionless and waiting.

It overlooked the valley and stream below, which was a good quarter of a mile from her home. This is where she came to escape from her four brothers and to enjoy the fresh air and to daydream in peace.

As the wind blew through her hair, she saw something shimmering and sparkling, maybe 60-80 feet away.

Rubbing her eyes to make sure of what she was looking at, she could make out a silver triangle shape hovering about 12 feet above the stream.

She immediately slowed the swing enough so she could jump off and then ran down the hill to see what it was.

When she got there, it was gone.

"*Where did it go?*" she wondered, as it only took a few seconds to get there.

Sharing this childhood story with me, she remembers it didn't make any sounds and had a light at each corner. She also estimated it to be around 10-15 feet long and was a silver metal material.

She also doesn't remember seeing any people around it and when asked about being abducted and missing time, she said she doesn't remember a sense of missing time or any strange dreams or memories.

She continued, that when she was 15-years-old and living in Stephenville, TX, she and her brother were out for a drive around town one night.

That's when they saw the sign for Rising Star, TX. They made the drive.

After driving for nearly an hour, she asked her brother, *"Shouldn't we have been there by now?"*

He agreed and offered to turn around and go back.

"Let's just go back," she said.

As soon as he turned the car around, they were immediately back in Stephenville.

During one of her dreams, you know, the ones that seem super vivid and real, she saw her brother floating motionless up at the ceiling while he slept.

Anna was standing in the middle of the bedroom and was in a conversation with a grey alien.

When she looked back at her brother, two greys went to get him. They lowered him somehow so they could move him around the room. One grey was at his feet and the other was holding his head.

Just then, a door or hatch opened on the floor and the two greys escorted her brother down into the hole.

When she was 34 years-old, she remembers having too much to drink one evening.

She recalls seeing a beautiful sunset in front of her, so she stopped to take a photo and then continued toward home.

While she was making her way along the curvy country road, she noticed an object in the sky pacing closely alongside her car. It followed her all the way home at the same speed she was driving. Then, once she got out of the car, she watched as it sped away.

"*I believe they were following me home to make sure I made it safely,*" she told me.

"*Many days later, while looking at the photo on my phone, there was something else in it. When you zoom in, it looks like a glowing saucer craft. That was the object that followed me home,*" she told me. "*I didn't see it when I took the photo on the way home.*"

She also has many memories or dreams of flying.

When asked if she remembers having or seeing a silver chord attached to her, like people having Out-of-Body-Experiences report, she said there wasn't one.

I asked if she was in a craft or flying like Superman?

"I was flying outside of a craft."

Chapter 22

Bigfoot Turned Into a Tree

Gifting in the Rocky Mountains

One summer morning a few years back, two friends, Dan and Josiah, went hiking deep into a canyon just outside of town. Their plan was to build a large tee-pee-like structure using fallen timber. It would be a gift to the area's Sasquatch people.

They arrived at their destination about 3 miles out of town and paused to look around. By the looks of things, they'd probably need to venture a bit higher up the mountain and deeper into the woods for enough material for the structure.

They blazed a trail as they made their way, adding another half-mile to the trek before they came upon a fairly level clearing with a tree stump near the middle of it. It was the perfect location for their gift.

They split up and started collecting skinny 10-15 foot tall timber to erect into the structure around the tree stump. The stump would act as a table within the tee-pee. The door or opening was about 5-6 feet tall. Once the structure was in place and standing on its own, they filled in gaps with smaller sticks, branches, and leaves to help keep the rain out. When they were done, they left a granola bar on the stump and headed back down the mountain.

After they arrived at their car, they packed up and began their slow drive back out of the canyon. Just when they were about to make the bend in the road, something moving up on the ridge caught their attention... and it was the ridge they were just on.

There, running on the ridge, was a reddish-brown haired Sasquatch, quickly making its way down the mountain toward them. When the creature reached the edge of the hill and saw the car, it stopped and just looked at them. As they looked back at it and as if it realized they'd seen it, it morphed into a tree, blending into the rest of the hillside. One second it was standing there and the next instant it was a small pine tree!

Was it a sort of defense mechanism or camouflage technique, used to remain unseen from prey and humans? It really didn't matter at that point, as they'd already seen it.

It would be a while after that before Dan went camping in that canyon. Everything seemed normal until one morning he awoke to find a small, light blue marble laying next to his sleeping bag. The marble had a piece of reddish-brown hair embedded inside it. What did this mean? Was it a gift from that Sasquatch?

Months later, Dan decided to venture out alone for an evening hike up another Forest Service road and then head off the trail to find a remote camping spot. As the crow flies, the location of this trip's campsite would be no more than 4 miles from the clearing him and Josiah built that tee-pee.

He didn't have to venture off the trail for too long before coming upon a nice level spot, perfect for his two-person tent. He was surrounded by tall trees which served to block out any noise from town, which was less than a mile below.

It wasn't long before camp was made, and his dinner was gone. For good measure, he backtracked through the woods to find a tree branch to hang a small bag of garbage. That would hopefully keep any nosy bears distracted and away from his tent as he slept.

Before turning in for the night, he pulled a canister of bear spray out of his backpack and grabbed a book for some light reading. Nearly an hour later, he rolled over and turned out the light and went to bed.

Sometime during the early morning hours, he was jolted awake by a deep rumbling feeling coming from the ground and the sound of a bulldozer crashing through the trees. It sounded like it was about 50 yards away and coming towards his campsite. The rumbling wasn't like an earthquake, but more like a stampede of horses or cattle running right at him. But how could that be? He was nestled deep in the woods and far away from the road.

He wondered, "*Were there free range cattle in the area and were possibly spooked or attacked, causing them away from a predator and unknowingly towards him?*"

As the approaching violence got closer and closer, his sleepy brain was simply overcome by the trembling ground and the loud crashing sound of the large trees right outside his tent. As he clenched his bear spray, he closed his eyes and braced for impact. Then everything stopped! Everything was suddenly quiet and peaceful.

He opened his eyes and focused his hearing, as he could sense something at the edge of his campsite to the left of his tent. There was no way he was going to look outside, so he continued to listen for any clue to what was outside.

It took less than a minute for whatever was outside to turn around and slowly walk away in the direction it came. Dan lay in his sleeping bag holding his breath. He could feel the heavy thuds from its feet as whatever it was walked away on two legs!

Needless to say, Dan didn't go back to bed. He couldn't sleep. He lay helpless as his mind replayed every second of the event over and over again, trying to make sense of what had just happened.

Come morning, he cautiously unzipped his tent and slowly and quietly climbed out of his tent. With every inch, he'd pause all body movement and hold his breath to scan to the left and to the right, before climbing further out. He was pretty shaken up.

Whatever it was, it was gone. There was no visible destruction within his campsite and, even more alarming, the trail back to the road was clear of any sign of the violence he'd both heard and felt. Even the garbage bag was still hanging from the tree.

Dan gave a lot of thought to what happened before telling me about that wild night. "*Whatever it was, once it found me asleep with the campfire put out properly, it turned around and let me be. I hadn't been making a lot of noise and my fire had been small, so I'm not sure how it knew where I was.*"

Dan wasn't the only one to have follow-up experiences.

During a solo afternoon hike, Josiah found himself about a mile or more outside of town, on the opposite side of town from where he and Dan built the tee-pee.

It was early evening when he set out. As he hiked parallel to a river, he eventually came upon a batch of similar tee-pee tree structures. They had been created by Boy Scouts and varied in sizes and distance from the trail. Hikers and campers used them as shelters. After he passed the first structure, he suddenly felt like something was circling him. It was such a strong feeling; it made him pause to look around to see if he could see anyone or anything nearby. That's when he felt the need to look down. There in front of his feet was an arrowhead, but it wasn't any normal arrowhead.

Josiah is part Native American and has seen a lot of arrowheads and knows how to make them. This one was different. Whereas they're usually created using a chipping or flaking method, this one seemed more like it was rubbed into shape.

By this time it was getting dark, so he hiked up to one of the tee-pees and climbed inside to rest and examine the arrowhead. While inside, he heard small stones being tossed at the tee-pee. He leaned over and stuck his head outside, but he didn't see anyone. The sound of stones hitting the structure continued, so he decided to take the hint and move along. Obviously, someone didn't want him there!

That's when things got a bit more strange. As he retreated back down the slope toward the trail, the stones continued to land all around him. At the trail and after stopping to look for the culprit once more, a large piece of tree bark suddenly manifested from thin air right in front of him. He said it wasn't there and then it was. He watched as it hovered in front of his face briefly, then fell to the ground. It was as if someone dangled it in front of him for a moment and then simply let it fall to the ground.

This freaked him out, so rather than continue up the trail, he decided to quickly backtrack toward town.

A ways down the trail, he realized he dropped the cap to his camera. Reluctantly, he turned back up the trail and used his flashlight to scan the ground ahead of him. Just as he spotted it and bent over to pick it up, someone threw something very large and heavy in his direction. When it made impact with the ground, he literally jumped and yelled, "*I'm just coming back for this!*"

Josiah then hastily made his way back into town and to his cabin. That was the last time he's hiked that area alone.

Chapter 23

Possible Abduction

Infection or Fetus Removal?

On the evening of April 20, 2010, a woman living outside Phoenix, AZ, felt drawn to look outside. When she did, she saw a circle of lights in the sky near her home, which grew very bright or intense and then disappeared.

She admitted all she remembers is it being solid black inside the ring of lights, and that it might have actually been hollow.

Moments later, strange lights appeared in her bedroom. She recalls falling down on the floor, but when she awoke some time later, she was lying on her bed. She added that after waking up, she felt sore inside and was very weak. She also noted having missing time.

Looking back outside, she saw four helicopters flying nearby, as if they were looking for something.

Afterwards, she fell ill and went to the hospital. She had become severely dehydrated and needed four bags of IV solution, and she had a 105 degree fever. Nurses told her all indications were that she had a bacterial infection.

Looking back, when the lights first appeared, she said she felt they were coming for her, and now she feels alone and empty inside.

Even though her housemates awoke from the lights and noises, nothing happened to either of them and when she tried talking to them, they simply listen and smile saying nothing.

In the days since this event took place, she reports still feeling weak and continues to have nightmares, where she only remembers seeing dark shadows walking around her before suddenly waking up crying, her heart racing, and also being short of breath.

When asked about her family's history of encounters, she said that, to her knowledge, no one in her family had any.

In many cases, family members have a history, whether discussed openly or kept secret, of abductions, contacts, or sightings. Memories of such events most often include sightings and missing time. Less often are memories of actual face-to-face contact, either onboard a craft or near the observer's home. Some even report having no interest in UFOs or are indifferent to the idea.

She added she considers herself spiritual and knows things, some of which she doesn't want to know. For instance, she said she knew what day her dad was going to die, as well as when she too will die. Once a spiritual reader told her an angel had visited her when she was 12 years-old.

Currently, she feels that her life will never be the same. She wants the nightmares to stop and is afraid to look out her bedroom window at night. She also wonders if some part of her is missing, as she feels empty inside and unable to explain why this has happened.

Chapter 24

Terrified of Contact

Retired Farmers Confront Fears

U nable to get enough, my two guests from Missouri returned for their third or fourth outing with me. This time, though, they requested a private tour, so they were the only ones going. I understood the reason for their request and it's exactly why we started offering private tours.

We welcomed thousands of people from all walks of life. This meant they brought with them their beliefs, religious backgrounds, prior paranormal experiences, as well as a wide range of fears. This created interesting and sometimes challenging group dynamics and is why we offered private tours.

For example, someone in the group may be fearful about close contact, but were okay with sightings in space. As a result, their fear discouraged or prevented closer encounters, which other people in the group may have wanted.

It's been my experience that those we were contacting knew everyone's fears and varied the group's experience as necessary.

Sometimes people just can't relax around people they don't know.

Therefore, the two people from Missouri wanted a private evening

Throughout this story, you will see examples of this play out. Even though the people involved may have said they wanted contact.

One example of what I'm referring to is when the group is watching an object move across the sky. Without fail, someone will ask, "*How do you know it's not a satellite?*"

Then, as if the occupants of the craft heard them, the object stops on the spot. Everyone in the group laughs and thinks it's funny.

The parked craft then falls to Earth right above us and appears to be a large ball of fire that's getting closer and closer. This continues until someone in the group says, "*Oh shit!*" Everyone's thinking it.

That's when the craft stops and goes back to resume its flight.

Yes, this has happened, and more than once. It's a real eye opener for those still on the fence about aliens and conscious communication.

Getting back to our ranchers from Missouri, earlier in the day when my guests came by to sign up for their private tour, I welcomed them back and informed them of our destination.

I asked, "*Are you two up for an overnight camping trip out there?*"

After a predictable silence, they both laughed and said, "*No thanks.*"

That evening, we sat on lawn chairs close to the locked gate and talked about their experiences back home on their farm.

They experienced unusual lights in the sky over their ranch. Their family and friends have similar sightings, too.

While we chatted, it occurred to me they might be ready to take the next step toward contact.

As we continued our conversation, I secretly invited those who were above us and unseen to come down and materialize their craft over the abandoned house behind us. I also asked that they come down low and center the craft over the house.

This was to show that they could in fact develop a relationship with those flying the lights they were so accustomed to seeing.

When I asked my guests if they were ready to take the next step, their response was, "*What do you mean?*"

I suggested, "*If you're ready, how would you like to meet the people driving those lights around your night sky?*"

Again, they asked, "*What do you mean?*"

I smiled.

"*It was as if seeing unexplained lights were all there was to it,*" I thought to myself.

Before answering, I looked to my left and noticed a black cloud over the house, only 10-feet above the roof. They also centered it over the house.

Turning back toward them, I asked, "*Have you noticed the cloud?*"

"*Yes. We wondered what it was doing there,*" the man answered.

It was pretty odd to have a cloud appear on an otherwise clear night, but to have a black cloud so close to the house was weird. This got their attention and was the whole point.

I then told them of my request as a demonstration for them. If they were content seeing lights in the distance, that was okay. But, if they were ready to go to the next level, our visitors were showing their willingness for closer contacts.

Seeing their hesitation, I reminded them, "*It's really up to you.*"

As they thought about it, I sensed they were not ready to decide and suggested they go home and await my email with the photos from our evening. I would include a link to a couple of guided meditations to help them proceed if they were ready. Again, it was up to them.

After roughly 15-minutes of discussion about contacting these beings and seeing this couple's reservations, I silently thanked our visitors for coming. The cloud then dissipated until it was no longer there.

Nothing else happened that evening.

About a year later, I received an email from this couple. They were back in town for several days and said they saw strange lights in the sky above their location. They asked if anyone else reported strange activities out that way. That's when I told them I had moved and was no longer in the loop.

As you can see, this couple wasn't ready to let go of the safety of those lights at a distance. It was comfortable for them and that's completely okay and is quite common.

In fact, many, if not most, of the people I took out could not handle much more than a passing light in the sky, which blinked when asked to. It was easy for them to discount the blinks as coincidence.

If it were to change direction or head toward the group, people started feeling uncomfortable and fear levels rose.

Their encounter with the cloud also shows that those in craft can hear our thoughts and may actually take part in ways not imagined. Coming down and materializing over the house in a manner that wouldn't scare them was a demonstration of their willingness to communicate.

The cloud being black made them think, *"How is that possible?"* and *"What does it mean?"*

A mother ship parked atop the house could have sent them running.

Jumping ahead two years, I ran into them at a week-long conference in another state.

"*Man, it's so nice to see you again, Todd.*"

"*Same here,*" I replied.

It was a Saturday evening, and I was preparing to take a group of 30 people out for an evening under the stars.

"*Are you two going on the sky-watch tonight?*" I asked.

"*Yeah, but we weren't sure about it. Now that we know it's you leading it, we'll be okay,*" he laughed.

The convoy of vehicles out of town was a long one, and I couldn't help notice the amazing sunset. There were a few clouds on the horizon to enhance the deep oranges and reds, but no clouds were above us or even in the area.

I thought to myself, "*The sky is great for a sky-watch tonight.*"

By the time we reached the location a few minutes later, that changed. Something was up.

With everyone gathered in a large circle, we all got comfortable and settled in. People sat on chairs, rocks, logs, blankets, and pillows, while a few people stood so they could keep moving to stay warm.

It's my experience that when a thick cloud cover appeared from out of nowhere, it's for a very good reason. Someone was too afraid and covering the sky in this way helped keep the fear levels down.

I realize this concept may be new to some people, but it happens and in such an immediate and profound manner that you have to step back and think.

During the 2-3 hours we were together that night, the clouds filled the sky and prevented us from seeing anything. We continued instead with questions and answers, as well as good old-fashioned storytelling.

Questions began about my personal encounters and then people dug in with questions about how it was done, how I felt when they arrived, etc.

Considering what happened with the clouds, I made it a point to discuss how group dynamics can play out during such a situation, as I knew some of them really wanted a ship sighting.

It comes down to each individual's attitude, belief, and fear. When joined with people who do not share the same beliefs, the results can be rather difficult to work with.

For instance, start out with two friends who want contact. Their beliefs, expectations, and energy are compatible as they are friends. When you add people from other countries, with different beliefs, religious upbringing, fears, etc., the outcome is going to be different.

When this happens, I use group meditation, drumming, storytelling, etc., to help sync the group's energy into a similar or more cohesive vibe.

This evening, I began by first explaining how objects reflect sunlight for an hour or so after sunset and again before sunrise. I refer to this as a reflective window, and it's how we can view metallic objects flying high above, such as satellites and even the International Space Station. It's pretty basic and everyone got it.

Next, I shared several personal stories of contact and others opened up with their experiences. It was nice to bond and answer questions.

That's when a woman said she wanted to have contact, but was afraid to go at it alone. She hoped to see something that night.

Then, someone sitting beside her leaned over and said, "*I can't believe you want to have contact. All I can handle is to have a light blink in the sky. That would be enough for me.*"

Comments and discussion like this continued. People began admitting their fears in front of others, even though they were all attending a five day UFO and Paranormal Conference.

In conclusion, and for those still wanting an encounter, I told them they may have an encounter during the rest of the conference. It could take place at home or back at their hotel later that night.

The evening ended and participants headed back to town.

One guy remained behind to talk. That's when I told him to look up. All the clouds vanished as quickly as they arrived. The sky was as clear as could be.

"*See what I mean about the clouds,*" I said.

The following morning, while checking in at the conference, I heard someone calling my name.

It was the man from Missouri. He and his wife were vendors at the conference and they were breaking down their booth.

When his wife stepped away to use the bathroom, he told me that later that night, after they came back from the sky-watch and were both asleep, he sat up wide awake.

"*That's never happened before,*" he confided.

"*In our room by the table, I saw a large green orb, possibly 1-2 feet in diameter. It was floating motionless in the middle of the room. Then, the object zipped across the room and appeared to vanish inside some sort of invisible slot.*"

He explained it as though the round light went into something with a flat edge and then was finally gone.

Then he admitted something I already knew. During the sky-watch that night, they were both afraid of what may happen and were glad to see the clouds come in. He had a feeling something would descend from the clouds, and that freaked him out.

While they weren't quite ready for a close encounter, he said they were afraid the space beings would still come close for those in our group that were ready for closer contact.

His green orb of light in their room was just another ball of light, but it was much closer than any of his other sightings. He was okay with that.

When he saw it, he said he wasn't afraid and suggested it may have had something to do with my presence.

He said, *"Just knowing you were here and that I trust you made all the difference in the world. I think that's why it happened, and I wasn't afraid."*

I laughed, *"But I was over an hour away last night when it happened."*

"Have you told your wife about it?" I asked.

"No, not yet."

Like I mentioned, sometimes when group dynamics are too crazy, contacts can take place when everyone's at home. In his case, in their hotel room.

That said, I suspect other contacts took place at the hotel for those that wanted them and were ready.

I've heard other researchers say that nothing happened when over six people were present. If they dropped that number down a body or two, that's when they saw things and had direct contact.

This isn't always the case though, as I've taken groups of 15, 20, even 30+ people out and had amazing things happen. You really need everyone in the same vibe.

In closing, after the week-long conference, I received an email from the wife from Missouri. Like her husband the night before, she too had a visitation in their hotel room. Her encounter took place the following night while he slept.

She wrote,

> *It was in the middle of the night; I was half asleep, half awake, and I opened my eyes and sort of in the same spot of the room that my husband saw the orb.*

> *I saw a black silhouette of a fairly large lobster/bug/Naked Lunch-type image with long legs, large body and it was all black outline, a solid black image floating in front of a small hazy florescent green fog!*

> *The image was like a cutout of a creature, not alive or moving. It was floating towards the ceiling of the room for several seconds.*

> *I continued to blink my eyes, thinking it was something in my eye or maybe I was imagining it to be something else… but it did not go away. Then, suddenly, it disappeared.*

This story, while it has many interesting facets, is about a retired couple from Missouri and their struggle to overcome fear. For him, he's still seeing orbs, but he's now okay with them coming closer. For her, she's seeing non-threatening shapes and even recognizable shapes.

Chapter 25

Life of Bigfoot Family

What if His Story is True?

W hat follows is a conversation I had with someone I met in a parking lot of all places. It is highly unbelievable, but if his story is true, raises some intriguing questions. Specifically, we already know Bigfoot are masters at blending into their environment, but what if they can blend into (our) environment too? For instance, what would they do for a living and how would they interact with neighbors? The *Munsters* and *Addams Family* TV shows come to mind.

One afternoon while grocery shopping in the city, I exited the store and made my way to my vehicle. While loading the groceries into the trunk, an approaching truck caught my attention. It looked like someone's work truck with their logo on the door. As fate would have it, they pulled up next to me.

The driver saw me looking at his business name and logo on the door. After he and his wife got out, I asked him about it. I won't give the exact name here, Cam, but it had the name Bigfoot in it. Specifically, I asked why he named his business what he did. He looked over at his wife and said they just had a child and the baby had pretty big feet for being a newborn.

I looked at him and paused... *"Oh, okay. I thought maybe it had something to do with Sasquatch."*

Then he looked back at me and paused... *"Really? Do you believe in Bigfoot?"*

"Yes, I do. I've interacted with them in five different states over the years."

"What do they look like?" he asked.

"Well, I've seen a couple of different types, you might say. The first type is the typical large hairy creature, and the second is well, very human like. They don't have much hair at all and look more like us than the first type. But they are still large like the hairy ones and have feet larger than ours."

I think this caught him off guard, as he looked away from me and over at his truck for about 10 seconds before looking back at me.

"You mean some of them can look like us?"

"Yeah."

He stared into the distance for a moment.

Then I asked, *"Have you seen one before?"*

Looking back at me, he appeared to be debating whether to answer truthfully.

"Well, I used to work for this man that was really big... I mean, really big and he had more body hair than normal."

"How big was he?"

"Almost 8 feet tall and he had a massive, muscular body."

He continued, *"Curious, I asked him once where he was from and he told me Alamosa, CO."*

"That's interesting," I replied.

"Interesting, why?"

"Well, those mountains outside of Alamosa have a long history of Bigfoot sightings. Maybe that was his way of saying where he was from without meaning the city of Alamosa. You know, Alamosa's the biggest town in that area. People may know of it and that would be enough."

He looked at me for a moment before continuing, *"You know, I also asked him about his shoes and clothes. Like, where he got them, as they were way bigger than anything I'd ever seen. He told me they are custom made for him and his family."*

After pausing again, he added, *"He shaved a lot, too. Like his whole body. He told me that too, once."*

"You know," he continued before collecting his thoughts... *"I once dropped a large tree off at his place and before leaving, said I'd help him move it with my tractor. He told me not to worry about it, that he'd take care of it. I didn't understand. He didn't have a tractor, and I was there with mine. It would only take a couple minutes, so I insisted and climbed down from my truck. He just looked at me and then walked over to the log and wrapped his arms around the end and lifted it up to his waist!"*

"What?"

"Yah, I still can't figure that one out! It weighed about 5 tons! He just picked it up and moved it with ease."

Smiling, I looked at my new friend and asked, *"So, did you really name your business after your son's big feet?"*

He laughed, *"No."*

This is where that conversation ended.

I realize many people believe Sasquatch is a beast, monster, and apex predator. Nothing more. However, there exist many accounts which suggest this creature is intelligent, compassionate, protective of their own as well as humans, and in many ways, human-like. Besides being humanoid, they have mates, rear children, grow old and die like us. Some accounts suggest they have different roles within their clan or tribe. They have also engaged in gift giving and other forms of curiosity and communication with humans. They may even have a sense of humor. Finally, witnesses report they look very human, and some hunters couldn't shoot it as it looked like a hairy person. Some Bigfoot have a face like a gorilla, some like a Neanderthal, and some very human like ours. Finally, there are accounts of people talking with them verbally as well as telepathically. Some have even received hand-written notes in English and drawings from the Bigfoot.

So, what if Bigfoot comes in several types, sizes, shapes, colors, etc.? Take dinosaurs, for example. Dinosaurs come in a variety of species, types, sizes, shapes, colors, and diets, but all are still referred to as dinosaurs. In the case of Bigfoot, might the same be true? It could account for all the varied descriptions and behaviors.

With all of this in mind, I'd like to pose a question: If someone claims to have spent time living with or among Bigfoot and if true, is it possible for Bigfoot to assimilate into our communities and way of life? Admittedly, reports of people being kidnapped by Bigfoot or going with them willingly are rare, yet accounts do exist. Could the opposite be possible?

What if this man's story is true?

Chapter 26

Tall Yellow Humanoids

Helping Mankind From Andromeda

This outing was large, with thirteen people, including two guides. The group was adept at meditation, and each person brought their own personal experiences of close contact and sightings. We all hoped for something interesting to happen.

During our guided contact meditation, and at the point where most people go deeper, half of the group noticed something, including myself.

Four people picked up one or more forms of contact. Several people smelled the fragrance of a rose; a few people felt a freezing chill only on a small area of their body. For me, it was only on the front of my face. Another person heard something flutter or wave around their head; and finally, someone else saw a tall yellow ET standing in front of him. In each case, the feeling only lasted for a moment.

The tall yellow visitor was in the middle of our circle and could very well have walked around, spending a moment in front of each of us.

Then there was the woman that fell back in her chair and lay motionless on the ground, as if unaware of her condition. When she got up, she asked what happened. She only remembered doing the meditation and didn't know how she ended up on her back on the ground. She was unhurt, and we all got a good laugh out of it.

The significance of the yellow ET is that right around the corner from our location was a special place.

Over the years, people have reported seeing tall yellow ETs with large round heads. One person shared with me she saw around 100 of them when she came out of a meditation in the canyon.

Upon realizing what they were, she thought to herself, "*Those are ETs.*" That's when they all turned to look at her in unison and seemed surprised she could see them.

They then projected a greeting message onto the rock in front of where she sat. The message showed they were from Andromeda and were here to supervise men in white lab coats who were working underground.

Chapter 27

Those Weren't Our Tracks

Campers Visited Once Asleep

T hree of us were camping at a local hot-spot. We stayed up until 3:30 AM before finally running out of firewood and getting cold. It had been a quiet and uneventful evening. My guests climbed into their tent and I took one last bathroom break before turning in.

I awoke to strange sounds several hours later. They were angelic voices. I also heard something in the bush outside the tent. That was most likely an animal.

The sun was up, so I got out of my sleeping bag and stepped outside.

The two others were still asleep.

As I approached our bathroom area, I couldn't help notice there was a wet spot in the sand in the shape of a perfect oval. Inside the oval were two footprints, or rather shoe impressions. The feet were smaller than mine and smaller than those of the two people still sleeping. I also noticed that the footprints didn't have a tread like you find on the bottom of boots or running shoes.

The prints were completely flat and without a heel. The strangest thing, though, was how the prints were inside the oval.

They were side-by-side, but the right foot was slightly behind the left foot. It appeared as though whomever did this was trying to keep their feet inside the wet oval. This made me look around the outside of the circle. There were no footprints leading up to the oval or away from it.

Once awake, I asked my guests if they left the tent that night, but they didn't. Nor had I, so who made those two impressions and where did they go without leaving more tracks?

We joked that someone came down to relieve themselves before beaming back up to their craft and continuing on their journey.

Chapter 28

Someone Pinched Her

Guardian Angel or Something Else?

During the drive to our destination, a woman said she was pretty intuitive and could pick up on the presence of beings and could read auras.

When we arrived at our first stop, I instructed everyone to set their chair in a certain location. This woman sat her chair near mine. I suspected there was more to talk about and as the evening went on, this would prove correct.

I overheard her tell her husband to take the camera and take photos to see if "*so in so*" would show up. I didn't catch the name she said, so asked her what she meant.

Her guardian angel appears in photos and she hoped to get a good shot of him.

When this didn't happen at the first location, she said she didn't understand. I suggested that the night was young and that he might show up at our next stop.

At the second location, I parked between the back gate and the driveway.

This woman's husband was riding shotgun beside me and after exiting the vehicle, he walked around the front of the truck and stopped to look around.

His wife sat behind me, and when she exited the vehicle, it was at the same time I did. Her husband was still in front of the truck.

She was unsure of something and told me she could feel the energy there and didn't like it.

"*It's strange energy,*" she said.

To me, it was more a matter of misinterpretation. Meaning, humans fear the unknown and this energy differed from anything she had experienced before.

After getting the gear out and providing a basic orientation or lay of the land, she told me that while she leaned against her door, someone pinched her side.

It was with such force that it pushed, or rather tucked, part of her shirt down inside the waistband of her pants.

Surprised at what happened, she instinctively thought she imagined it because nobody was within seven feet of her. Until she looked down and needed to pull the shirt back out.

This terrified her, so I reminded her of our previous conversation about her guardian angel.

The simple fact is, things, and I mean strange things, happen there almost every time we visit. It's in such an environment that I believed her angel could reach out to her like never before.

Chapter 29

Levitated Above His Bed

Imagination or UFOs?

While lying in bed one evening, he wanted to levitate above his bed.

"*I don't remember the exact reason for this, but I recall something about going on board a spaceship, as if they beamed me aboard,*" he told me.

"*Stirred up from a recent movie or conversation? I really don't remember.*"

He continued, "*While lying on my back and with my eyes closed, I focused on lifting higher and higher off the bed. Then it happened.*"

"*I felt a strange sense that I was about 6-inches above my bed. I don't know how long this sensation lasted, but when I was ready to open my eyes to see if it actually happened, I was still flat on my bed.*"

"*That was weird,*" I remember thinking before sitting up to look out the window and up at the night sky.

"*The following morning, after I arrived at work, I noticed the computer network was down.*"

"*Network services that were always available were mysteriously shut down and nobody could figure out why,*" he laughed.

"*Odd as it was, I thought little about it after that.*"

"*An hour later, a man that worked with the local police department entered my office,*" he said.

"*I told him that his data was not available because of the network outage. He commented, 'I* wonder if it has anything to do with the UFO sighting last night.'"

"*I asked what he was talking about and he said they received multiple reports of a UFO over the area the night before.*"

Chapter 30

Surrounded by Invisible Coyotes

Meditation Reveals the Unseen

During a training tour, I took the new guide out to a hot-spot to show him around.

When we got to the contact meditation part of the training, he asked to sit inside the truck to keep warm. I started the truck and turned on the heater.

We followed the visual guidance in the meditation. Having done this meditation many times before, I knew that at the 3/4 mark, things start to happen. I was curious to see what he would detect or feel.

Sure enough, the surrounding energy changed towards the end. Once finished and while still in the thick of things, he said he needed to go out and stand beside the vehicle.

He closed his eyes and was silent for a moment.

Then he said, "*They are all around us right now. I can see them.*"

Then he went silent again.

He lifted his arms away from his side and then slowly up to shoulder height. After pausing, he moved his hands inward to touch his chest. The instant his fingers touched his heart, coyotes, and a lot of them, started howling.

They must have been right at the edge of the driveway and surrounded us. They were that close.

The howling and yelping continued for a minute or two before stopping suddenly. They all stopped at the same instant - every one of them in unison.

Now that didn't seem right to me. He thought this odd too and started barking to illicit a response. Nothing. Utter silence fell upon us and we never heard another peep.

When we got back into the warm truck, I asked him what he thought of the meditation and what impact it had on him.

He told me it amazed him at how powerful it was, and especially towards the end.

Because of how it kicked in, he needed to get out and stretch. As he was doing this, he sensed many beings around us and, with his arms up and out, he tested them.

Speaking in thought to them, he told me he knew they were there and apologized for doing his test anyway, but he wanted confirmation that he could see or sense them.

He asked them for a sign of their presence as soon as his fingers touched his heart. Not before and not after, but only then.

This is when he started moving his hands towards his heart. Once they touched his chest, the coyote music started. Then, when he thanked them in thought, they stopped.

Chapter 31

They Know Our Thoughts

Just Curious or Dangerous?

Two women from Europe came out with me and we ended up standing in front of the main entrance to an abandoned home.

The gate is a heavy pipe construction and swings on hinges toward the left side of the driveway. There are three padlocks and a heavy chain securing the right side of the gate, with enough slack to allow the gate to move about a foot while locked.

One woman leaned against the gate and looked up the drive toward the house. Hoping to see something, she took several photos.

Her friend was twenty feet or more from her and to her left. I was even further away, toward the end of the driveway.

While leaned against the gate, she thought to herself, "*It would be so easy to crawl under the gate and go up to the house.*"

At the exact moment she finished that thought, something or someone pushed the gate toward her with such force, it threw her backwards and away from the gate.

She couldn't believe it. Looking around, she thought it must have been me, but I was walking up the driveway toward her when it happened.

This isn't the first time someone picked up an unseen being near the gate and tried to get a photograph of them.

On other occasions, we've heard a squeaky door open and close from the house. It's as if they knew we arrived and came out to check on us. The sound of footsteps soon followed the squeaks.

Chapter 32

The Floating Boxes

Ships Visit Remote Canyon

With no tour scheduled for the evening, another guide and I took a drive back to our favorite location to see if anything was out there.

We neared a stop sign and, as we slowed, we noticed two bizarre clouds hovering over the canyon. There were no other clouds in the sky, but that's not the strangest part.

These clouds were the size of a house and were rectangle in shape like shoe boxes. They were perfect three-dimensional rectangles with flat sides and right angles. Then, in a failed attempt to hide, the outside of the boxes had dark and light gray cloud cover as a camouflage.

We stopped at the hiking trail-head and got out for a better look. They parked side-by-side right above the resort, a stone's throw from where we stood. These objects were at the cliff's edge and hovering 50-100 feet above the top of the rock formation.

With no time like the present, we jumped back in the truck and headed for a hill around the back of the mountain.

When we got there, they were still over the mountain.

I grabbed one of the green pen-lasers and started blinking at them, as if saying, "*We know you are hiding in there.*"

That's when the cloud covering dissipated and within 15-seconds, they were completely invisible. We knew they were still there though, but if you never saw them, you'd never know two ships were hiding above the mountain.

Another time, a strange looking cloud was close to us. All the other clouds were moving in the wind and looked normal. But this one didn't budge. It even looked like a large spaceship.

Watching it for several seconds, a friend said he was sure it was a cloud-ship. Taking his eyes off the cloud for a moment, when he looked back at the cloud, it had moved across the sky to a point some distance from where it was. In its new location, it again floated motionless.

He watched and waited, but saw no movement. He had to look away once more and when he turned to check on the cloud, it was back to where it was the first time.

"*Someone is messing with me,*" he said as he laughed.

He no longer doubted the possibility of a ship hiding among the clouds.

Chapter 33

Star Trek Over Malibu

Not All Clouds Are Clouds

I t was time to wake up. I was sleeping in my car during a road-trip and the winter weather was cold and wet.

That's when I received a telepathic message telling me I needed to walk down to the bottom of the mountain and wait for their signal to return.

I did not know what this was about, but reluctantly followed the instructions.

The day was growing longer and longer and I wondered when I could return to the top of the hill where I was parked. I was cold and tired.

Then something told me to look back in the mountain's direction and when I did, there was one of the strangest clouds I have ever seen.

It looked like the Enterprise from Star Trek, but that's not the strangest part. There were two of them, positioned head to head as if the one were floating in front of a mirror and the second was the reflection.

The tail end of the craft was the strangest part of the cloud. It was checker boarded with gray and white squares. At the end of the cloud, it appeared to blur and fade out.

The entire thing was comprised of cloud stuff, not only the checkerboard out back. The mirror effect actually comprised the entire craft, so there appeared to be two of them floating face to face.

While examining the cloud, the nose solidified, and its underbelly glistened in the late afternoon sun. Almost as if part of it were metallic.

In amazement, I thanked them, and it morphed back into a normal cloud.

Ships acting as clouds are not uncommon. Many people see them and I've seen many over the years, but this one took the cake.

The next day, a triangle-shaped cloud was over the mountain. It had sharp angles and sharp edges. No puffiness.

Chapter 34

Those Weren't Real People

Strange Canyon Hike

During this warm spring evening, two women brought their puppy along on the outing. It was a fun time. On the way back to town, we stopped at one of the area's trail-heads. The time was 11:30 PM.

With a thirsty puppy, one woman took care of the pup while her friend and I looked up at a rock formation.

I used a green laser pointer to draw imaginary squiggles in the air and on the cliff walls, when out of nowhere, a small glowing saucer-like craft descended behind the rocks. After we made zig-zags with the lasers, the craft zig-zagged as it descended and before disappearing inside the mountain. Were they mocking us or trying to get our attention?

The women asked about a good place to go hiking with their dog. They were staying in town for a few more days, so they'd have time to explore.

The first location I recommended was right where we were when we saw the saucer go behind the rocks. There are many amazing and true stories which come out of that area. Not only is it full of trails and canyons to explore, it is also where the black helicopters and men in military uniforms are sometimes seen.

The other hike was in a small canyon around the corner.

They set off the next morning intending to hike both trails… but as I soon found out, that didn't happen.

Hiking the first trail, they noticed a large area filled with strange rainbow colored rocks. They made a mental note to stop there on the way out take photos and explore the area, but that didn't happen either. Upon their return, the rocks were no longer there.

Several other things happened.

1. They saw strange appearing people walking the trail with them. Their 4-month-old puppy acted strange when these people came around. They said the puppy never acted that way before.

2. Using two different cameras, they took many photographs, but while near where those rainbow colored rocks appeared, the photos didn't save on either camera. Images shot before and after entering the area were fine.

3. In one photo, there appeared to be strange fuzziness around one of their faces, while everything else was clear and in focus. They checked the lens for smudges, but it was clean. No other photos on their trip had this fuzziness. This one photo was near a tree where one woman thought they saw a strange light emitting from the center of the tree.

Experienced hikers, they said they were moving the entire time, not sitting or napping. They were at a loss for what took them so long to reach the end of the trail. It took many hours, while it took them about 30 minutes back.

"Something happened to us in there," they said.

Wondering what may have happened, one of them suddenly remembered having drank water off a rock near the trail. Their dog even had some. Everything strange began after that, they said.

They also recalled feeling very fatigued and dehydrated, but noted that they always bring a lot of water. This trip was no exception. Then, at one point, they felt totally refreshed and revived from such a serious lack of energy. This allowed them to exit the canyon.

Because of the missing time, they never made it to the second hike.

Chapter 35

Another Time Slip

College Student's Experience

Arriving at our second destination of the evening, we gathered everyone around and handed out flashlights for the short hike. About 10-15 minutes later, we were all looking at the farmhouse.

Everyone huddled along the property fence, wondering what would happen next. I reminded them to be open to various attempts to communicate with them via their five senses, not just their sight. Some of them were more serious about this than others in the group.

To get everyone's attention and pull them together, I told them about a tour guest who once had 3 hours of missing time. Everyone checked their watches.

One man gasped and shouted that his watch was not correct when it was earlier that evening. Everyone gathered around him to see that he was missing 3 hours. He swore he did not change his watch, which I should add was a wind-up analog watch, not digital.

Arriving back at the van, he called me over to look at his watch again. It reverted to the correct time during our hike back to the vehicles.

Adjusting the driver's watch rather than someone else's, actually made more of a statement.

He was the driver, and it was his duty to meet everyone else at specified times during their trip. If his watch was incorrect, then it would be bad.

It would have been cool to see the hands of his watch spinning forward and backward. Likewise, to know the exact location along the trail, those adjustments took place.

I haven't heard of many episodes of missing time during my tours.

This made me curious about what it was like, so one day I asked if *they* would create an experience for me so I would know.

The following week while on the way to a friend's house, I rounded a bend in the road and headed up a short hill. As I approached one of the side streets, I said to myself, "*There's Small Canyon Road.*" A mere moment later, my head and body shook as if adjusting in my seat. It was minor, but enough to get my attention.

As I continued around a bend in the road and then crested another hill, I said to myself, "*There's Small Canyon Road.*"

I immediately recognized what had happened and started laughing, thanking them for the experience.

They moved me, in a blink of an eye, back down the road about a quarter of a mile, allowing me to repeat my earlier actions. That was pretty cool.

Chapter 36

It Flew Into a Portal

Always Sit Shotgun

Our tour was over and we needed to get back to the shop. It was late and the young couple in the truck with me had to get a good night's sleep before leaving early in the morning.

Cruising around 20 mph down the dusty dirt road, up ahead was another canyon, and then we would hit a paved road. We could then make better time getting back.

Both the boyfriend and I were looking out ahead of the truck when it happened.

Up ahead, we both saw a white streak of light or an object shoot upwards at a 45-degree angle. It then disappeared into a flash of bright white light. The object appeared to vanish into a portal.

The craft flew out of the canyon and once it was around 1,000 feet above the ground, a bright white portal opened for it. The portal closed or disappeared after it went in.

This all took place in about 1 second. The girlfriend in the backseat didn't see it.

Chapter 37

TV Film Crew's Encounter

Mischievous Ghosts?

When a TV network came to town, they were skeptical, but were open to hear about our experiences. They were filming a family outing with us.

As for sightings in the sky, nothing much happened. We spotted one or two unknowns overhead that weren't on our satellite report, but no ships appeared or came low for the film crew. But there was some rather strange activity taking place on the ground.

I was unaware that the camera crew hiked a way's off to set up a time-lapse camera. Later that night, I spotted a strange red light behind our group and approached it to see what it was. That's when I saw the camera. It was pointing down at the ground as it took photos. I didn't understand why they'd do that.

While back at the store, I asked one of the crew about it. He told me it surprised them and that they couldn't figure it out.

The rig was top quality and so strong, he said, that when they left it for the night, everything was secure and locked in place. There was no way it could have moved by itself.

I should add that whatever their motivation to run time-lapse in that direction over the mountain, several of us had sightings in that area and the film crew knew this.

Could it be possible that someone moved their camera so their craft or activities wouldn't be caught on film?

As described in the previous chapter, we witnessed an object flying out of that canyon before disappearing into a portal. We've also watched as two craft exited another portal near that location.

The second mystery of the night happened while one of the TV crew was holding our night-vision scope and high definition video device. It included a small video control module with a display screen to hold as you record.

The crew member was recording the family when I noticed a bright flash on the display. The video display blanked out and then returned. He thought nothing of it, but I knew something was happening.

During several previous tours, this happened and at the exact moment it did, something or someone was perceived in the area. More than one person sensed this.

What I am suggesting is that this camera is susceptible to certain electromagnetic anomalies and that an unseen being may have, in fact, passed by the cameraman when the flash occurred.

I've been in known haunts and had this phenomenon happen to the camera.

Could it have been when someone messed with their time-lapse camera, making it point at the ground?

The last unexplained event involved the producer and his smart phone.

All day long and throughout the tour, he was busy texting messages and emailing someone. Work obviously distracted him and it's my guess someone else may have noticed as well.

The sky-watch part of the tour was over and the family was getting ready to leave. The rest of us had to break down the equipment and pack it away before we could leave – and this included the film team.

I noticed one of the night-vision sets was missing and so was one of their crew, a former Marine. I mentioned this to the producer, and he seemed to be aware of this.

Several minutes later, the Marine was back in camp and appeared to be looking for something. The boss' smart phone was missing.

Using the night-vision goggles, he located it some distance from the group and behind a large bush. The producer never walked in that direction, so how it got there is anyone's guess.

Chapter 38

It Watched Us

Invisible Being Shows Up in Photo

"*I want to see a UFO,*" they say. Yet, it often comes down to fear they are unaware of, which prevents them from seeing a craft. Over the course of their night out, those fears come to the surface so we can deal with them.

The mother's fear of something caused an immediate blanket of clouds above us. They weren't there all night, then suddenly and completely covered the sky when we started talking about contact.

We discussed fear and how someone up there was aware of her fear. Rather than scaring her, they rolled out the blanket of cloud cover to lesson her anxiety so we could continue.

"*This has happened before,*" I said, "*so don't feel bad. It's a way for you to recognize there is something causing your fear and to show you they are sensitive to that. Now you can go home and discover what's causing your fear.*"

Before ending the evening and heading home, I offered to take a photograph of both of them using night-vision goggles.

The daughter wanted one with the mountain behind us in the background, while her mother wanted to stand *"over there, next to that bush,"* as she pointed.

Something in the photo by the bush baffled me for more than a month. It was the figure of someone standing behind them. It was a dark silhouette off the mother's right shoulder.

When I showed them the photo, the mother said she actually felt a presence near the bush and is why she selected it for her backdrop.

One benefit of taking photographs with night-vision equipment is to see into the unseen. For example, night-vision goggles don't just see in the dark. They also see into the Infra Red light spectrum, which our eyes cannot see. The being in the background was invisible to the naked eye, but showed up in infrared.

Mom knew someone was there, but couldn't see them. Now she had proof.

Someone visiting this location with me previously said that this area is a major thoroughfare for beings in other realities, both above and below ground.

Chapter 39

Butterfly Leads Lost Hiker to Safety

Winged Insect or Spirit Guide?

It was early evening. I parked in the parking lot some distance from the river and meandered along many of the trails until I came upon the river.

I had never been there before, and with my thoughts all over the map, so to speak, I wasn't focusing on any one thing, let alone where I was going.

I rested on the bank of the river with my feet in the cool water, when an otter swam by.

When the otter disappeared around the bend in the river, I decided I should head back as well.

I stood up and looked back at the edge of the trees. I knew the general direction to walk, but I would need to find the right trails if I wanted to get back before it got dark.

I neared the treeline when I came upon a fork in the trail. I thought to myself I wasn't sure which direction to go.

That's when a butterfly appeared inches in front of my face. It fluttered so close to me I could almost feel the brush of its wings, as if it were trying to get my attention. It worked.

It fluttered towards the trail to my right, so I went that way too. That's when it vanished.

I continued in that direction until I came upon another fork in the trail. Again wondering which way to go, the butterfly appeared in front of me. This time, it fluttered off to the left along the trail and I followed. A few steps on my way, I noticed it vanished again. I believed it was there to help me find my way out of the woods.

Before long, I approached another trail. Without thinking, I went right and looked around for my friend. I didn't see him.

Then, at my next fork, I stood there waiting. This was a test. As soon as I thought to myself, *"I don't know which way to go,"* the butterfly reappeared and led me to the main trail.

That's when I knew where I was.

Rather than head back to my car, I took a detour so I could sit on a nearby deer trail. I saw some deer up on a ridge moments earlier and figured they would head down toward me on that trail. I sat quietly just off their path and waited.

Thinking I needed help, my butterfly friend reappeared and seemed to want me to head back to the trail. I looked at him and laughed.

In my mind, I sent him this thought: *"I know, I know, but I want to stay and wait for the deer. I will come out once I see them, I promise."*

He fluttered back up to the trail, and I turned my attention back to the deer to my left.

Sure enough, four of them came up over the crest where I sat and they froze the instant they saw me. The young deer leading the way looked at me and turned back. He went off their trail by about 10 feet and then walked around me. Once they were all out of sight, I got up and went back out to the main trail.

There he was, fluttering to my right and waiting. I thanked him and headed up the trail to the parking area.

So was my new friend really a butterfly or something else?

Many cultures believe in life-after-death. Because the caterpillar transforms from a ground-crawling creation into a creature that flies, the butterfly is oftentimes revered as a spiritual sign.

For example, ancient Aztecs believed the dead returned as beautiful butterflies to visit their relatives and assure them all was well.

What if someone died in these woods and appeared to help me when I didn't know which way to go, thus ensuring I didn't succumb to the same fate as them?

Chapter 40

The God of Wind

A Bizarre Event

As with many of my experiences, it's likely nothing would have happened unless someone else was there with me.

In this example, a young woman from Japan was visiting town.

After meeting with a local psychic, she learned she should go to a popular rock formation outside of town. It was one of the more famous formations and believed to house an energy vortex.

Having been on a tour with me the previous night, she returned to the store and asked to talk to me. She wanted to know if I'd take her to that rock formation.

At the time, we weren't doing day tours, and I used the downtime to do other things. She pleaded with me, so I agreed.

I went back to my desk to get my things and when I returned, one of the other tour guides had walked in. She couldn't have timed her arrival any better.

I asked her to join us. I soon learned she took part in drumming ceremonies at that rock formation. I asked her to guide this trip, and she accepted. It was a nice change of pace for me and I enjoyed the idea of just tagging along.

Our first stop was an area tourists know little about. It's an area the Native Americans use for their ceremonies. Next, she led us to a trail which winds its way down to the creek behind the mountain.

As I followed, I picked up something. Someone insisted that I take a photo and in which direction. I looked where they were showing me, but saw nothing out of the ordinary.

Again, I felt it was important to take a photo, but I didn't do so. I ignored the voice because I saw nothing with my eyes. I should have known better and wish I took the photo so I could see what the fuss was all about.

About an hour later, we looked at the clock and told our guest we needed to get her back for her next appointment.

We made good time getting back to the front side of the formation and to the location where I didn't take the photo.

Curious, I surveyed the side of the canyon wall to see if I could spot anything unusual from that angle. Nothing and no one was insisting I take their photograph.

Then, without warning, we all froze in our tracks at a thunderous sound coming from the top of the mountain. The three of us stared up several hundred feet to see what was making the noise. It sounded like a military jet's afterburner.

After about 10 seconds, the sound subsided to the point we could no longer hear it. We then looked at each other and shrugged our shoulders. None of us saw anything in the air, let alone a jet flying overhead.

Again, without warning, the sound returned. This time, it shook loose many of the smaller rocks at the top of the mountain. They rumbled their way down the side of the cliffs and crash at the bottom ahead of us. Another 10 seconds and the sound stopped. It was at that point we hastened our hike around the bend and back to the car.

That's when the most bizarre thing happened.

Ahead on the trail was a flat rock bridge, like what you might see at a waterfall.

Once all three of us stepped onto the bridge area, a mini tornado came out of nowhere and engulfed the three of us. It was crazy.

Our bodies were being rotated, and our backpacks sucked upwards. Then it stopped.

It didn't seem like a dirt-devil, as it came from within the rocks and sucked us into it. There wasn't any color to it either.

The two of us guides looked at each other, laughing and using expletives to describe what had happened. Meanwhile, our tour guest had stepped backward away from the flat rock we were standing on. She was speaking in Japanese and asked us to wait a moment.

When she finished putting her camera away, she stood up and told us that while living in Japan, some amazing things happened to her. When she asked a psychic about them, she was told that when she's in special or important places, the *God of Wind* speaks to her.

That was, in fact, not the first time she experienced something like this.

That only generated more laughter and expletives with our hands in the air. Our tour guide grabbed the girl and gave her a huge hug, saying, "*You're my new best friend! That was amazing!*"

Now, going back to where I felt compelled to take that photo and refused, I still don't know what or who was there talking to me. It was, though, in the same location the God of Wind spoke to us.

During another tour, our group hiked to the dome above a cave. At one point, I felt a similar need to take a photograph, but it wasn't as insistent as with the God of Wind.

I stopped and looked down at the rocks in front of me. All I saw was a strange shape in the rock. It looked like a vertical piece of stone. I snapped the shot and walked off to look at other areas.

When the tour was over, I took the couple back to the store and I drove home. As I reviewed the photos on my computer, I couldn't believe my eyes. The vertical piece of stone was more than a piece of stone, it was someone's nose.

Right there in the rock was the face of someone looking right at me. Was that who called out to me at that moment and told me to take their photo? I know it sounds too fantastic and far-fetched, but it had to be. There was no one else there and I know what I heard. In the photo, you can even see the whites of their eyes.

It's because of this, I again wished I had listened and taken at least one photo at that rock mountain. It was definitely one of the strongest or most insistent feelings to do so I've ever had, yet I refused it.

So, how often are we spoken to or receive guidance, but do not recognize it or listen?

On another occasion, while driving in Colorado, I noticed a large saucer-shaped cloud in the otherwise clear sky. I heard, "*Take a picture*" and I did. Then, once I rounded a bend, I looked back, and the thing was gone.

How about animals reacting to impending earthquakes and tsunamis far before human technology? How do they know?

Did you know scientists discovered an immediate reaction to sun flares in bacteria here on Earth? Yet, it takes humans eight minutes before we know about it using our best technology?

Chapter 41

It Entered His Bedroom

John Wayne's Ghost?

A popular vacation property once frequented by the late Marion Robert Morrison, also known as John Wayne, was being managed by a friend. When she mentioned needing a website to help promote stays, I offered to help her.

My work included a new website with fresh photography and a promotional video.

Using a high-definition video camera, I began by taking short video clips of each of the rooms.

Everything went smoothly until I entered the bedroom above the kitchen. Something was making the camera flicker and distorted the video recording.

It could very well have been due to out-dated electrical wiring in the room, creating an EMF (electromagnetic field). Other areas around the house showed similar disturbances on the video. Something was happening in all three bedrooms within the main house.

When I told the property manager about it she shared several stories of how guests reported paranormal activities in the house. Those reports pertained to the same three bedrooms, but couldn't be explained away as EMFs.

Most recently, one guest reported hearing footsteps coming across the great room toward his bedroom as he was in bed for the night. Curious, he sat up and watched as the doorknob turned and the door opened. No one was there.

Another account was how a guest was in a different bedroom brushing his teeth in front of the bathroom vanity. Suddenly, and for no reason, the toilet next to him flushed.

In the bedroom upstairs, where I originally experienced a disturbance when filming, things moved around the room while people watched.

Admittedly, walking through parts of the home, you can feel someone watching you.

Chapter 42

The Clouds Parted

Weather Controlling Aliens?

Right before sunset, a large van full of university students pulled into the parking lot. There were a dozen of them, and they were all about having a good time. At least that's what we thought when the doors opened and students and smoke rolled out.

When we reached our first destination of the evening, everyone gathered their chairs in a large circle.

After giving them a brief orientation, someone fired up some Pink Floyd.

A couple minutes later, three people came up to me and began asking more personal questions. They were genuinely interested in how to make contact.

I asked the others who were playing the music and talking if they wanted to have contact. If so, they would need to minimize distractions and clear their minds.

I began by explaining that all that is necessary is for them to request contact and be open to some form of response.

To begin, I asked everyone to observe a moment of silence and, in their own thoughts, extend their desire and willingness for contact.

At that moment, everyone agreed and wanted a sighting, but the cloud cover was thick and covered the sky above us.

Within 15 seconds, a large circular hole opened in the clouds above us and in that opening, a shiny object zipped by. Everyone noticed the opening in the clouds, but not everyone saw the craft that was visible.

Then, after thanking them for this display, the hole in the clouds closed, and the students discussed what had happened.

Chapter 43

A Conversation With a Crystal Skull

Henry Meets the Scanners

The first time I used a cordless RADAR detector was while hiking atop a large rock formation.

I sat the device down on a nearby rock as I surveyed my surroundings and rested. About 15 minutes later, two friends approached, and we shared in the moment together. They carried with them an identical device, but had it powered off.

One of them pointed out a cloud in the distance which looked like a letter X. When we noticed the cloud and spoke about it, my detector chirped. That was the only time it made a sound while up on the rock.

Later that afternoon, while driving down the highway, we had a device placed in each corner of the dashboard. We joked about sharing our chocolate candy with the ETs. As we laughed, one of the two detectors began a rhythmic and low tone chirp that actually sounded like a laugh. It laughed with us. All the while, the second device, also powered on, remained silent.

That got my attention and not for the laughter. If radio waves sent out from a police officer's radar gun registered with one detector, it would have set off both devices, not one.

In the days and weeks to follow, I used the detectors in various locations during tours. I suspected that within the unseen world, or outside the electromagnetic spectrum frequencies we refer to as the visible light spectrum, something or someone may communicate with us using the radar detectors.

While out in the desert late one evening, we positioned four of them around us. One was in each of the four cardinal directions to detect contact and from which direction.

If someone wanted to get our attention, they could interact with tour participants in a whole new way. It could explain the laughing sounds heard previously.

One evening, two of the tour participants were off-duty police officers. You can imagine the look on their faces when the radar detectors came out of the bag. They did not know what was about to happen.

Once the chirping and laughing began, they had no choice but to look at each other and scratch their heads. They even stepped away from the group for a moment to talk it over. They believed it was a hoax, but couldn't explain it.

I should add that these devices produce unique beeps or chirps, depending on the radio frequency band detected. When these things go off in the middle of the desert at midnight, it's not just one chirp here or there. Every sound they can make, we hear, often bouncing between X-Band and KA-Band chirps, for example.

During another tour, I stood in front of two people while holding one device in each hand. They were on, but remained completely silent.

I told them how they work, what sort of things have happened with them, etc. That's when they began sounding off. Then silence, which was more like a long pause.

During the pause, I told them that one time the alarm associated with X-Band was going off in one hand, but not the other. The sound coming from the second device was for KA-Band, and nothing else. Then, after a moment of silence, they switched sounds at the same moment.

Most likely doubting what I told them, the radar detectors in my hand did just that. It even surprised me. I thanked those unseen in my thoughts for sharing with us in such a way.

The one on the left was making a distinct alarm sound and the one on the right a different sound. Then they both paused for several seconds and switched sounds. The device on the right changed its tune to what the other device was playing, and vice versa.

How is this possible? You can see why the police officers scratched their heads.

While visiting friends, I brought out the radar detectors to see what would happen at their home. They chirped and beeped a few times before falling silent.

My friend introduced us to her good friend Henry, a crystal skull she brought home from Egypt.

I placed Henry beside the devices and see what would happen. Within seconds, it was as though they began talking to each other. The beeps, chirps, tones fired up and wouldn't stop. They were so loud, we couldn't continue our own conversation, so I put them in time out.

Henry went on the table next to the house while the chatter-boxes went onto a small table in the backyard. Not a peep was heard for nearly an hour while my friend and I talked.

When finished with our conversation, I grabbed Henry and walked him over to the table and sat him in front of the radar detectors. Nothing. Not even a beep.

Wondering what was wrong, it occurred to me they were pouting or respecting our need for silence while we talked.

That's when in my mind, I thought, "*I'm sorry we needed to separate you guys. It was getting loud, and we wanted to talk. Thank you for understanding and you can now continue your conversation.*"

At that exact moment, they began chatting away.

For someone who's never seen it in real life, it's amazing. Having even one detector present during a conversation can illicit laughter and strange tones not normally heard from it.

This begs the question, "*Who's on the other end doing the talking?*"

A little while later, the dogs started growling and made a fast run for the corner patio and started barking.

I walked over to see what got their attention. Not far away were six dark objects between the house and the river. They were small recently planted trees, say 4-5 feet tall.

Hearing all the excitement from her dogs, my friend came out to see what was happening. I pointed out the dark figures to the left and asked her how many she counted. Six. We both counted six.

About 10-15 minutes passed when the dogs quieted and retreated to their cushions. I looked back and counted only five trees this time. I called my friend back and asked how many she counted and this time it was five. Whatever was out there had left. She'd even commented how she could see a ship close to the trees.

Chapter 44

Strange Humanoid Encounter

Secret Base or ET Vacation Spot

A former employee told me she worked at the hotel for a year and during that time, saw some strange things.

One was a man who walked funny, as if not quite human. She saw him several times, but one morning and out of curiosity, she approached this stranger and greeted him with, *"Hello."*

The stranger stopped and mechanically rotated his head towards her.

"It was as if he were a robot," she told me.

"He paused before scanning down and then back up my entire body. When he finished scanning or whatever he was doing, he continued on his way. He never said a word and his eyes were not normal either. They were all black."

Then there is the appearance of tall ETs in area canyons and resort areas.

During one of my evening tours, a woman in the group told me a group of ETs communicated a message to her.

She said, "*They told me they are from Andromeda and are supervising the research by men in white lab coats working underground.*"

A different woman said she saw three ETs standing on top of a rock in the canyon and were looking at us while we were in the parking lot below.

Asked if they are doing secret military operations, she said, "*No, they are on a different mission, but they wouldn't elaborate.*"

Chapter 45

You're Not Alone in There

Single Mother's Shower Encounter

I magine being a single mother with three little girls in a small mountain town looking for a new place to live before winter.

They had been living in a fifth wheel RV trailer with her brother and his dog, about thirty minutes away from her job. Winter was on the way, and they needed a place to live that was closer to work, and fast.

One day, she came up to me all excited, *"I just got the keys to a new place!"*

"Where is it?" I asked.

"It's just down the road at the lodge," she beamed.

"It's a 3 bedroom, 2 bath apartment and I'm so happy."

"Which apartment?" I asked.

"Apartments 1 and 2, with an adjoining door."

Then, without thinking, the following words just came out of my mouth: *"Those units are haunted."*

She froze, and her excitement left her face.

"*Don't tell me that!*"

"*Sorry,*" I said, putting my hand over my mouth. I didn't want something else to slip out and totally ruin her day.

"*What do you mean?*" she asked.

"*Well,*" I said, "*there has been ghost activity there for a long time.*"

Then she asked, "*What sort of activity?*"

"*Housekeepers, maintenance workers, and even overnight guests have reported certain things,*" I answered.

"*For example, bone chilling cold spots appeared suddenly next to more than one housekeeper while they were cleaning.*"

"*Also, I remember a rude couple that wanted to check in late one night. After their room was ready, they complained it was too small, and they wanted something larger.*"

"*When morning arrived, I heard them in the office demanding a full refund.*"

"*Once they left, I asked the owner what happened.*"

He told me, "*They complained about the second apartment being too cold all night. In fact, they said they nearly froze to death all night long and none of the extra blankets helped. Evidently, they even kept all their clothes on too.*"

"*Then they made a mess of the firewood out front and even destroyed the cover, trying to get to the wood. Supposedly, they couldn't get the fireplace lit and the thermostat wasn't responding, even when pegged at 90 degrees!*"

I interjected, "*That apartment was hot last night when I checked it.*"

He agreed, "*I know. It was hot this morning too when I checked the heater.*"

Looking back to the mother of three, "*Whatever happened that night, it appeared they weren't welcome and were made as uncomfortable as possible,*" I told her.

"*Additionally, the ghost or ghosts have been reported to venture from apartment to apartment along only one side of the building.*"

She responded, "*Oh okay, so it's nothing sinister or anything bad then. I can live with them as long as they're not trying to scare me and the girls. I've had enough of that kind of stuff.*"

The very next day, after she moved in, she couldn't wait to talk with me.

"*So I lit a candle on the kitchen table and sat the lighter down. When I returned to the kitchen, the candle blew out and the lighter was nowhere in sight. I looked everywhere for it,*" she added.

"*Then, while sitting on the couch, I could hear a man and woman talking in the apartment next door. I couldn't tell exactly what they were saying, but I distinctly heard a man and woman in conversation.*"

"*It was weird,*" she continued, "*That apartment is empty. No one is living there. I even went to the neighbor on the other side of that apartment and asked if he's ever heard anyone talking next door.*"

"*He had, and on more than one occasion,*" she told me.

A few more days passed, and she found me again.

"*Guess what just happened?*" she joked.

Laughing, I said, "*I give, what?*"

"*Last night after taking a shower, when I opened the shower door and stepped out onto the mat, I saw a large hand print on the mirror!*"

She continued, "*It wasn't there after any of my other showers. I put my hand up to it and it was much larger than mine.*"

Then I remembered to ask, "*Did you ever find the lighter used to light that candle?*"

"*Yes,*" she said. "*I found it a few days later by the stove and behind the trash can. I was the only person in the apartment when it disappeared.*"

"*Now that's weird,*" I laughed.

Then she added, "*As soon as I picked it up, I felt a bone-chilling cold that gave me goose bumps and the shakes – it was that cold!*"

"*What did you do then?*" I asked.

"*I left them alone and went into another room.*"

"*Later, when I returned to the kitchen, that cold was gone.*"

I gave her a week before asking her if anything else had happened.

"*Yes,*" she answered.

"*Now someone's hiding my car keys and my boyfriend's asthma inhalers. I put the keys in the same place and after I turn my back, poof, they're gone. They have taken two of my boyfriend's expensive inhalers, which his life depends on. So that's not funny at all. To this day, he's never found them and now keeps an inhaler in his pants pocket. I look everywhere for my keys, but only find them in an obvious place once the culprit wants me to find them.*"

I let her know that of all the times I've been in that row of apartments over the years, I've experienced nothing. Not even the cold spots, but I've heard a lot of stories.

That's when she showed me a photo from inside one bathroom.

"*When you close the door behind you, there are sideways claw marks or scratches on the door frame, and lots of them, as though someone or something tried to get out of the room while laying down.*"

"*If an animal, like a dog, were clawing at the door or door frame wanting out,*" she added, "*some or all of the marks would be vertical, right?*" she asked.

"*All of them are horizontal to the floor and go up about 24-inches above the floor, and none are on the door,*" she said.

"*Yah, I think you're right,*" I said.

"*I can't think of anything that would claw up the trim in that manner.*"

I added, "*When I was around 5 years-old, I had a recurring nightmare where I would wake up in the middle of the night and upon hearing voices in the living room, walked into the kitchen and toward the living room. When I got to the doorway to the living room, some unseen force always stopped me and pulled me backwards by my feet. Each time, I grabbed at the door frame with both hands while laying on the kitchen floor. I remember screaming as whatever or whomever was behind me pulled me back towards my bedroom. My screams always went unnoticed and no matter how hard I resisted, they wouldn't allow me to cross over into the living room.*"

"*In such a situation,*" I continued, "*it might be possible that I left horizontal scratch marks on the door frame, not wanting to be pulled backwards, but again, those were only dreams.*"

"*Is there anything else I should know about?*" she asked.

"*Well, over the years I lived in half a dozen different units there and only one was so bad, I couldn't sleep and had to move to another apartment.*"

"*What do you mean?*"

"*Well, it didn't matter how tired I was. As soon as I got in bed, I was wide awake and never fell asleep. I don't remember exactly how long I stayed there, but it wasn't long. I moved out and could sleep in the next apartment.*"

"*Oh my gosh,*" she exclaimed, "*my boyfriend and I are having problems sleeping too.*"

"*We've also heard someone walking around up on the roof,*" she added, "*but that's not what's keeping us awake. It's something else, like something we can't audibly hear. We can't put our finger on it.*"

I clarified, "*Yeah, I'd stay in the living room on the couch until I got tired, then go to bed. Then, without fail, I would lie in bed wide awake and full of energy all night.*"

I added that at the time, I thought there may have been a strong E.M.F. running through the room, but wasn't sure. I only learned of the ghostly activity months later.

A few days later, I saw her at work and asked, "*The other day, you mentioned being okay with the ghost activity, as long as it wasn't bad. What did you mean?*"

"*We better sit down for this one,*" she laughed.

She began, "*As a child, I saw a lot of strange things at home and at my aunt and uncle's. A lot, you might say, was demonic.*"

"*Our family was Christian, attending church service every Sunday, so there is no history of seance or Ouija board activity.*"

"*Getting to the stories, once my mother, myself, and one of my cousins awoke with scratches down our backs. As best as we can remember, the activities only took place when there was no man in the house. In a way, the men were there to protect us, even if they didn't know this. It attacked us when the men were away.*"

"*My parents both had their own closet in their bedroom. My father's closet was always ransacked, no matter how clean he tried to keep it. Someone or something always messed it up. My mother's closet remained untouched. It only happened to him.*"

"*Even now,*" she added, "*my father is very organized and yet, things disappear only to reappear days or weeks down the road.*"

"*Most recently, my mother sent me a text saying that some of dad's books have flown off the bookshelf by themselves.*"

"*Another time something kicked me out of my bed when I was 15 or 16 years-old. They hit me in the gut with such force while I slept that*" my body folded in half and I flew onto the floor. I was the only person in the room. Whatever it was, it made a sound like big wings flapping. The room was dark and I couldn't see anyone specifically, but I noticed a dark shadow above me. I was terrified to stand up, so I crawled out of the room into the hallway. It's weird that I didn't think to wake up my mom to tell her what happened. I turned on the bedroom lights and just sat in bed."

"My aunt and uncle's house was so terrifying, us kids would dare each other to spend the night in their house. None of us ever went down into the basement, as we could look down the stairs into the darkness and see darker figures moving about. We also heard strange noises, besides the usual water heater or plumbing noises. Us kids were terrified to even go into the laundry room, which was how you accessed the stairs to the basement."

"For example, one time my uncle heard his 4-year-old little girl screaming. Running into the living room, she was being drug around the room by her hair. His baby girl was the only person in the room."

"They moved into another home up north, closer to the mountains. No one slept upstairs. After seeing shadow figures and hearing footsteps in the hallways, everyone slept downstairs. They also heard knocking at their door every night, but nobody was ever there. We also saw figures walking through walls."

"One time at this same house, I saw a rose outside in the wintertime. My aunt photographed it using one of those instant Polaroids. When the image developed, there was something else in the photo. It looked like Jesus and he held up one of his hands so we could see the nail mark."

"A younger cousin talked to someone invisible, often being overheard by my aunt, but she thought little of it. Then one day an older lady came by to visit. She explained that her and her husband used to live there and *that he passed away in the house. She wanted to reminisce a bit and even brought a photo album to share with my aunt and cousin. While flipping pages, the boy pointed out her husband and said that was his friend he's been talking with upstairs."*

"Then there's the man seen looking in my aunt and uncle's living room window during the day. Whenever they checked outside, they never saw him. He also appeared while it was snowing, but he left no footprints in the snow. My aunt and uncle never learned who he was."

"I would also sometimes see a tall being in our house. He always stood with his back to me, so I never saw his face. He was also floating and even glowed a bit, like an angel might. Because he wore a purple robe with white and gold fringes, and had a gold crown, I refer to him as the King. When he was present, nothing bad happened. Streaks of bright light were also present and sometimes went into the wall. During these encounters, I felt calm and safe."

"One night, I awoke to see a dark figure of a man in my closet. That paralyzed me," she said.

"This last experience happened a few years ago. After my grandmother passed away, one of my brothers got her old cow bell. It was old and rusty, weighing in at around five pounds. It was heavy-duty. Because it was so heavy, he displayed it in the cabinet in the living room. Then the obvious happened. Someone jolted everyone awake in the middle of the night by ringing her bell. After that, he got rid of it."

"Grandma always said she was going to haunt us."

Chapter 46

She Won't Go Into the Kitchen After Dark

It Mimicked Her

In the 1950s, a small Catholic chapel was being built in the woods at one end of the long mountain valley. The Church's plan was to have the priest move into a recently built house up the hill overlooking the chapel.

The priest welcomed the community into the beautiful new chapel, which looked like the one from the TV series "*Little House on the Prairie.*"

The community welcomed him with open arms and filled the small chapel every Sunday morning. Everything went well for the first couple of years. That's when members of the parish noticed things went missing. For whatever reason, people suspected the priest.

They accused him of stealing from the both church and the community. Rumors spread throughout the area communities and he was no longer welcome. He denied any wrongdoing and even claimed that many of his belongings went missing as well.

The Catholic Church removed him and let the parish remain closed for a while to let everyone calm down before they assigned a new priest. The home on the hill remained unoccupied for seven years.

The Church made the new priest live somewhere else, so they could put the house up for sale.

A family from Michigan purchased it sight unseen. They loved it and quickly began raising their three children.

Before long, they too noticed some of their things vanished. Occasionally, they even saw objects moving by themselves on tables and shelves.

Still living in this house, one of their daughters told me the following story:

> *One night around midnight, my mother awoke with a dry mouth and went into the kitchen for a glass of water. As she lifted the glass of water to her mouth, she noticed something moving out of the corner of her eye.*

> *Something was moving outside behind the house and was being picked up by a security camera.*

> *My mom lowered the glass and walked over to the TV screen, which displayed video from the security system.*

She said there were two floating lights several feet above the ground. As if performing some sort of dance, they rolled and flipped over each other in a frolicking or dancing sort of way.

After watching them for a few moments, she said to herself, "What are they? They're not bugs…"

At that moment, the lights stopped moving and hovered for a few seconds, as if now aware that they were being watched.

That's when the two lights merged and became one. The light then moved closer and closer to the house until it stopped right in front of the camera.

The light then morphed into a human woman, and it looked like my mother! She said it was like looking into a mirror. Startled, my mother jumped backwards. The being outside did the same thing, as if mimicking her.

My mom then pointed at the screen and yelled, "Now you stop that right now!

Upon doing this, the being in the camera vanished and she's never seen them again. In fact, none of us have.

I asked if the lights ever returned.

"*No. To this day, my mom refuses to go into the kitchen at night. She's afraid that if she does, the lights will return.*"

Chapter 47

School Field Trip to a Cemetery

Kids Raised in Haunted Town

I will be the first to admit this one is strange: Taking young children to a cemetery as part of a school outing?

The previous day, while leaving the grocery store, I ran into one of the local school teachers.

She asked me if I knew any ghost stories for our town.

"*My class is taking a field trip to the cemetery tomorrow,*" she said.

"*If you have some good stories, I would love you to join us and share them with the kids.*"

I remember thinking, "*Halloween is next week, so maybe this is something they'll enjoy. Otherwise, it's kind of creepy, even for me.*"

Later that night, she emailed me that the Principal and the parents were okay with the idea.

"*Alright everyone, come sit over here in the shade. Todd has some ghost stories to share with us.*"

I began, "*I have seven stories about ghosts and if we have time, I can share some local Bigfoot sightings with you.*"

A roar of excitement erupted from the group.

"The first story is about a place called the Villa. Do any of you know where it is?" I asked.

They shook their heads, saying no, they didn't. A few of them said they had heard of it before, though.

"While preparing for bed one evening, a woman was upstairs in the master bedroom preparing for bed. While washing up, she placed her wedding ring on the counter. Though her husband had passed away several years earlier, she still wore the ring."

"In the morning when she awoke, she noticed something next to her out of the corner of her eye. Her wedding ring was sitting in the center of the pillow next to her."

I reminded the kids that she was the only person staying in the house.

"Housekeepers have reported ghost activity while cleaning as well."

"In one instance," I added, *"the housekeeper was washing dishes when someone ran across the large dining room toward them. Startled, they turned so see an empty kitchen and dining room. They were alone in the house, so what or who was in the house with them?"*

The children gasped.

"I've been in this house," I told them.

"The floors are tile in that part of the house, so you can imagine how loud the running footsteps must have been."

"During another incident, a different housekeeper was dusting in the living room when he heard noises coming from upstairs. When they went to investigate, he found a light turned on inside one of the bedroom closets. It was off earlier and now it was on and the coat hangers were swinging back and forth."

"*At the same time they reached out to stop the swinging motion of the hangers, the bedroom door slammed shut. The closet light also turned off all by itself, which freaked him out even more. He flipped the bedroom light on and tried to open the door to leave, but it wouldn't open.*"

"*Luckily, he had his phone with him and called his boss at the office for help, telling them to hurry.*"

"*The bedroom door opened.*"

"*What happened?*" asked his boss.

"*Let's go,*" the housekeeper yelled, as he ran down the hallway for the front door.

While at lunch, he told his boss everything and said he wasn't going back after lunch.

"*I am never going back in that place again.*"

From their expressions, I could tell the students were loving this story.

I continued, "*The first time I went inside the Villa, I was with a group of others. There were twelve of us, and we were there to see if anything paranormal would happen. And it did.*"

"*As soon as we opened the front door and stepped inside, we all heard cabinet doors close in the master bath upstairs. That's the same bathroom the woman left her wedding ring on the counter.*"

"*Nothing more happened for at least an hour. We all split up, with someone camped out in every room and the lights out. We remained silent and listened and watched for anything unusual. Nothing.*"

"*Then someone downstairs on the couch took a photo with their cellphone. In the photo, something large and white streaked across the room above our heads.*"

I let everyone catch their breath.

"*Okay, the next story is from the Fun House. Do any of you remember the carousel?*" I asked.

Everyone blurted out a resounding, "*Yes!*"

Of course they did. It was an indoor amusement park with a roller rink, pool tables, arcade games, restaurant, putt-putt golf, and much more.

"*One evening while making his rounds, the closing manager was turning off the lights around the building when he passed by the carousel. That's when it started back up. Music, lights, and all.*"

"*He turned it back off and walked across the room to the ice cream machine. That's when it started back up. Thinking there was a power surge or short in the power cord, he unplugged it.*"

"*All was well until he unlocked the back door to go outside. That's when it burst back to life.*"

"*The machine was still unplugged,*" I told the kids.

"*I heard the employee quit, but I don't know who it was to confirm that.*"

The kids looked at one another and laughed.

"*Are you ready for another story?*" I asked.

"*A couple of you may already know about this cowboy story, as your parents managed the bar where it takes place.*"

I was looking right at the two girls in front of me.

"*Ask your dad when you get home if you don't believe me,*" I smiled.

"*This story is about a ghost who enjoys a stiff drink at the local watering hole. People sitting at the bar sometimes claim they saw an old dusty cowboy sitting at the end of the bar.*"

"*He never speaks, but seems aware of people talking to him.*"

"*Then there's the story about Crazy Charlie, who used to live in the tiny cabin down the road from the bar.*"

"A couple I know were visiting friends who were renting the cabin."

"In the far corner sat an old, dusty recliner. Nobody knows how old it was or how long it's been in that corner."

"The girlfriend told me her boyfriend sat down in the dusty relic and got comfortable. That's when the chair flipped over backwards with my boyfriend still in it."

"Out of the corner of her eye, she told me she thought she saw Charlie laughing."

I asked the kids, *"Do any of you know who Crazy Charlie was?"* No one did.

"Okay, this story is about an old miner wearing pajamas and slippers as he walks down the back road over there."

"Anyone ever seen him or heard about him?"

Some kids thought they had seen him, or it was some other stranger walking late at night on the same road.

One boy said he was once out past midnight with a friend. As they walked along the right side of the road, a shadow person in the shape of a man walked the same direction on the left side of the road and kept pace with them. They said hello to him, but got no response.

"Alright, here is the last story. It's a crazy one, so make sure you're sitting down."

Still sitting down in front of me, they all laughed.

In conclusion, I told them about the Catholic Priest's problems and the girl's mom who refused to go into their kitchen after dark.

Chapter 48

Deer Chased by Gorilla

It Jumped a Two Lane Highway

A friend shared this encounter with me recently. All the years we've known each other, I never knew this happened.

He began, "*One afternoon while heading back home, I made my way through the canyon and out of nowhere, a deer bolted across the highway from my left to right without slowing or looking. It was as though it was fleeing for its life.*"

"*Knowing deer often travel together, I slowed down thinking another deer might be coming. I also wondered if I might get to see what was chasing it.*"

He looked at me and smiled. "*You will not believe what came out of the woods after the deer.*"

"*It happened so fast. The deer sighting, me pulling off the highway… Then it appeared from the trees.*"

"*What was it?*" I asked.

"*It looked like and ran like a gorilla, on its rear legs and then down on all fours.*"

"*Like the deer, it didn't seem to care that I was there. This predator focused on its prey and, with one long jump, landed on the other side of the highway and was in the woods in pursuit. It happened so fast and right in front of my parked car.*"

"*It cleared the entire highway,*" he said.

"*It was dark brown and had yellow eyes. As it was about to launch across the road, it looked at me. That's when I saw its eyes.*"

"*I am 6-foot 2-inches tall and I figure that when this thing stood up straight, it was at least 1-2 feet taller than me. It was also really broad, with massive shoulders. His arms were long too.*"

"*It happened around 8 PM. To be honest, it was shocking, and I told myself nobody would believe me.*"

"*Even telling you now is giving me goose bumps.*"

While talking to him later, he told me he's only shared this experience with one or two close friends.

Chapter 49

The Sleep Over From Hell

The Dog Watched in Horror

A t sixteen and while living in San Antonio, TX, April's friend asked her to spend the night.

"*I knew better,*" she told me, shaking her head.

"*She has been my friend since grade school,*" she continued.

"*Over the years, I saw the abuse she went through first hand. Something evil was haunting her house, or was coming for her.*"

"*For example,*" she said, "*my friend often awoke with scratches, bruises, and even bite marks all over her body.*"

"*When she finally invited me to spend the night, I did not want to, but she was my friend and needed my support.*"

"*The one and only night I agreed to stay over, I awoke in the middle of the night with something on top of me. Its grip was strong and I couldn't breathe. It was choking me. I couldn't see it or pull its hands from my throat.*"

"*How did it end, or how did you get it to stop choking you?*" I asked.

"*It took a moment or so, but I remembered to invoke the Lord's Prayer.*"

She continued, "*Because I couldn't breathe or speak, I had to recite the prayer in my thoughts and out loud as best I could. That's when it let go and vanished.*"

I asked, "*Did it also attack your friend that night or at least wake her up while attacking you?*"

"*No. She somehow slept through it. Her dog knew I was being attacked, though, and could have even seen the creature, but I couldn't. The dog was freaking out and barking and growling aggressively, but could not help me.*"

"*And your friend could sleep through that?*"

"*Yes. I don't know how, but she did and when I told her what happened, she cried and hugged me, apologizing over and over.*"

"*Her parents had enough and moved to another city. I only saw her at big events like the State Fair a few times or during summer vacation.*"

Curious, I asked, "*Did the attacks on her continue after they moved?*"

"*Not that I'm aware of,*" she said.

"*I asked her the last time I saw her, and she said no, but that was a long time ago.*"

"*Going back to your attack,*" I asked, "*did you spend the rest of the night at your friend's or did you go home?*"

"*No. I went home. There was no way I could stay there. I even told my friend that I was sorry for leaving her.*"

"*I was too disturbed and unable to sleep. I made the long walk back to my house. While taking a shower later that morning, a sharp and piercing pain traveled down my back. Something or someone had scratched me.*"

"*I never want to go through that again!*"

Chapter 50

Vampire Creature Hunts Deer

Chupacabra or Something Else?

"**I** own a hunting lease in Texas," the man began.

"When I built my small hunting cabin, I included an observation deck on the roof to shoot from."

"Before sunrise, I grabbed my rifle and climbed the stairs to the roof. While sipping my morning coffee and watching the deer grazing below me, I thought I heard something."

"Moments later, I heard it again. Whatever it was, it was behind me and was breathing."

"Spinning around, I saw a strange creature sitting on the edge of the rock cliff behind my cabin. It was watching me."

"My guess is that it was using the high vantage point to hunt the deer below. From the cliff and the roof of my cabin, you could see several hundred yards across a large field," he added.

"The creature was about 3 feet tall, didn't have any hair or fur, and its skin was a dark gray. Its eyes glowed red, like they were back lit. The red wasn't a reflection or eye-shine."

I asked, "*What did you do?*"

"*Well, it was nothing I'd ever seen and I've hunted all my life.*"

"*I reached for my phone to take a photograph, but I must have left it downstairs.*"

"*I got up to go get it and all the while, it was staring at me.*"

I asked, "*Do you have windows on the back of the cabin that you could see it from?*"

"*Yes, and when I looked up to see if it was still up there, and it was watching me.*"

"*When I got back on the roof, it was gone.*"

"*Did you ever see it again?*" I asked.

"No," he said, "*but I asked around about it.*"

"*What do you mean?*"

He replied, "*Us hunters go to breakfast in the morning and while gathered in the lodge, I asked around if anyone's seen anything strange.*"

"*That's when the ranch owner approached me, smiling.*"

"*Yes, several hunters have photographed an unusual creature.*"

He continued, "*It's not dangerous to us, at least so far. It goes after small game and has been here many years now. We're not sure what it is, exactly.*"

That's when I told him, "*It sounds like the legendary Chupacabras. I've heard they attack and drink the blood of livestock and other animals.*"

"*It sounds like it was up there stalking the deer before you arrived,*" I added.

"*That's kind of creepy too,*" I said. "*That it watched you descend into your cabin and when you looked up at it through the window, it was looking back at you.*"

Conclusion

Thank you for reaching the end of this book! If you enjoyed it, please leave a review on my Amazon book page.

As I continue to meet people willing to share their experiences, I will document them for you to enjoy in future books of this series. Book two is already well underway.

If you would like to access the playlist of podcasts for many of the stories in this book, you can either visit

www.ParanormalBedtimeStories.com

or scan this QR Code with your smartphone. You will be prompted for the following password: 8 6 7 5 3 0 9

About The Author

In 2006, one of Todd's friends shared a story of a woman in North Hollywood, California, who took people up on her roof to see UFOs. She suggested that maybe his experiences and insights were to prepare him to do the same.

"*Absolutely not,*" he insisted.

Even though he strongly opposed such an idea, was shy and an introvert, that's exactly what he did a short two years later. Well, sort of...

A couple of years later, Todd accepted a Tour Guide position, taking participants out at night to facilitate paranormal contact. But after nearly two years of nightly outings, teaching others how to make contact, and then build relationships with other beings, he needed a break and retreated to a life of quiet solitude in the mountains.

Todd is originally from the American Midwest. He has lived in Europe and Asia, and has traveled through many countries and nearly all the USA. Along the way, he's met interesting people and heard some of their fascinating stories. Many of which are included in this book.

While in Africa, Todd met a special woman. Their supernatural love story is the subject of another book, so stay tuned for that.

He is also working on a fiction title, which he hopes to publish in 2024.

To stay informed of future projects, Todd's book website is

www.ParanormalBedtimeStories.com

Printed in Great Britain
by Amazon

15472910R00139